365 Days of Truth Volume 2

Kelly Logan

Published by Better By Intent Publishing, 2023.

While every precaution has been taken in the preparation of this book, the publisher assumes no responsibility for errors or omissions, or for damages resulting from the use of the information contained herein.

365 DAYS OF TRUTH VOLUME 2

First edition. October 4, 2023.

Copyright © 2023 Kelly Logan.

ISBN: 978-1971255064

Written by Kelly Logan.

Table of Contents

365 Days of Truth Volume 2 | Days 1-50 1

Days 51-100 23

Days 101-150..45

Days 151-200..67

Days 201-250..83

Days 251-300... 105

Days 301-365... 127

Extras because that is how God rolls! 151

365 Days of Truth Volume 2
Days 1-50

1.

It is easy to live in God consciousness when everything is going good but why is it when something starts to go sideways we forget our center, God, and start grasping humanly? God is ever available where you are for all need **but you have to remember to let God flow.**

When things start going wonky I used to feel the frustration welling in me, either I was trying to do too much or trying to do beyond my capability but determined to make it happen because of my ego. Fast forward to now I still get that prickle of irritation, you know that feeling, a flush or tingle, but I rest back for a second and stop. If I am frustrated that means I am of man's thinking mind and not God consciousness. I bring to mind a Truth, usually "your will Father, not mine."

To give it up to God, his will, his way allows me to back down from the old road and take the right road where I just drive while God navigates. It is truly freeing once you get into the swing of it. Once you give up control you wonder why sometimes you forget and try to take it back.

2.

The Tree of Life bears eternal fruit.

3.

Everyone gets sick, why? They believe in the law of germs which is *belief* not Law or Truth. Therefore the reason for all *disease* is a universal *belief* in a law that **doesn't exist** that results in illness and death in the human experience. This is the mesmerism or hypnotism human man believes therefore experiences as reality.

4.

There are many opportunities to remind yourself of the presence of God. Whenever you sit down to eat or grab a cup of coffee you are missing the opportunity to give thanks for the grace that has been presented to you as the bounty of the Father.

Say thank you Father at every occasion. It might be for a parking spot, a squirrel not getting squished on the street as it darts across traffic, thankful for the baby and mother enjoying a stroll in the sun. All is God. Learn to see past appearances and see the Source, the Truth of all creation and realize you too are of that creation and take your place beside the Father as joint heir to the kingdom and all the fullness there of.

You must truly understand what you hold in your consciousness is nothing short of infinite supply unto your existence because you are of God and if you know this, acknowledge this and live in this atmosphere of oneness with God your existence is lived out in the loving embrace of the Father's promise that all will return home but until then you are to enjoy heaven on earth letting God bring Life and abundance to you as its expression of peace, health, joy, abundance and benevolence.

5.

The just and the unjust, the righteous and the unrighteous.

There is no God holding you in bondage to your sins, you are being held in bondage *by* your sins, ie the sin punishes the sin, what you sow so shall you reap, what goes out comes back.

Your violation of spiritual Law is what creates the conflict within you, not God. God knows nothing about your human life because *human* man is not of God consciousness because *human* man is not God's creation. *Human* man is nothing more than a visible form of ignorance thought to be Truth. There is no thing called *human* man created by God but there is that which is *named* human man that is no more and no less than spiritual man ignorant of their true being and labeling themselves as that which is separate and apart from God, that which is material in nature and not spiritual in nature which is the Truth of all.

6.

To partake of God, to be joint heir of God you must **express as** the child of God.

You cannot be in violation of spiritual Law and in communion with it at the same time. One is of man and one is of God and cannot express in the same place at the same time. To be the child of God you have to express as the child of God and that is deferring to the Father, letting God go first and being an instrument of grace to the world. It is silently, sacredly and secretly bringing the allness of God to those asking for God, for change, for another chance, another choice.

You become the wayshower to awaken others by your knowing God aright and are the first true base of a spiritual movement no one will know about unless they hear it from God within when it is their time to start their journey home set in motion by your knowing God to share God.

7.

The difference between man who choses to rise above humanhood and man who wants to stay in humanhood is the man who choses to rise will at some point stop suffering the things man suffers and at the same time have been enjoying the things of God more and more.

There is a light at the end of the tunnel but you have to start walking toward it now if you are ever going to know where it is coming from.

8.

"Father forgive them and open their eyes that they may see."

Don't worry that in forgiving them their offenses you are setting them free from their punishment. It doesn't release them from the culpability of their actions it merely brings God to bear in the situation. All offenses are done under the law of man and must be met out by the law of man.

When you repent, know Truth and rise above the error you made you are completely forgiven, there is no sin, no stain on you in the eyes of God. To the eyes of man you may be looking at some serious time or consequence. Many wonder why if they are forgiven they still have to suffer the consequences of their actions.

Each time you feel error coming back to bite you is a chance to repent, stop being human and return to God. Most of the time our errors start out small as are the consequences but there are always consequences. If you are like me when I suffer a consequence of my action it feels icky, heavy and I back the heck up and bring about a healing. I hate getting stung by humanhood and it hurts more and more each time because I freaking know better!!! But the good news is you course correct quickly and all is good. **The suffering was the reminder not to go and be human again because it sucks.**

When you open yourself back up to God after falling for duality God does not know you were gone therefore it does not lessen or in any way alter, affect or diminish the reality of your spiritual union with God. You missed out on some quality time with God and there are things to atone for in the human world for your little jaunt outside of heaven's gate but keep God consciousness while you attend to what is needed to fix your human mistake and God will be the Law unto the world as you do your community service or make amends. Do what is due Caesar, do what the law of man require while keeping your consciousness with God for guidance and harmony.

Every choice determines your now, your present circumstances. By letting God direct your life you are guaranteed to be spiritually supported because with God navigating the bus you are not picking up the sword thus harmony is the Law unto your expression and within that Law is Life eternal.

9.

It is foreign to man's nature to go to God **within** the silence of their own being to **feel** the presence of God, the harmony, the peace, the joy that oneness brings but it is only through this desire to know God that all the added things come into your experience as miracles in your midst.

10.

In reality you aren't looking for a God to fix your problems, you are looking for the state of being you can live out from of which harmony, peace, joy and abundance are the only expressions and that is only found in union with God consciousness which is achieved by listening for the voice of God within your own being.

11.

Spiritual understanding may consist of a lot of words in teaching it but it consists of very few words in living it. Everything and I mean everything you are learning is done in silence. Everything you are experiencing is experienced in the silence, everything you are receiving you are receiving in the silence and everything you are expressing is expressed in silence for silence is a principle of Truth.

12.

This that you do with your mind, the reading and studying, is merely a preliminary step to prayer, inner listening, which is done in consciousness. This inner listening is the flow of grace from the within to the without to bring harmony into your experience and the experience of those of like consciousness ie open to that which is unseen but called upon for support in all ways.

13.

You can only find that which you seek.

14.

A life well lived is one of **your** choosing and not that of other external/world/human expectations or perceived forces.

15.

You can only benefit by what you know to be Truth and Truth is within your own being experienced as peace, understanding, healing, rest and joy.

16.

The only thing God can give you is what it **is**-harmonious expression by the harmonizing of **your** expression, all of it. This means the harmony of God becomes your harmony as you practice, study, die daily and nothingize error.

Take note, the harmony you receive is God's harmony not man's. This can take the form of losing a job because the more correct one is ready for you, the person you love may be released from your current experience but it is only for the formalizing of harmony unto **you.**

A relationship may be one you think you love but it also may cause feelings of fear, anxiety or other negative emotion that are in the way of God level harmony. Remember this is only about you, your harmony because it is your desire. God cannot harmonize anyone who does not desire it and this means those extraneous to you cannot be harmonize by God just because you want it.

However, God's grace through you as harmony may mean you find yourself alone ie the person has left, not because of you but because

God's harmony for you means without that person in your consciousness and it is only then that the next step on your journey can come into expression. When you are on the spiritual path **you have to just let Life play** out around you because it is moving and shaking you to where you can start progressing beyond your current expression.

But you have to let it happen, ie not beg someone to stay, not compromise yourself for another because you are afraid of *what if.* If you are with God the what if is **God harmony.** Do you see the difference when God is running the show? Yes it is going to suck at times because there are emotions involved, the knee jerk reaction to hold onto that which you know you should let go but if you just keep putting one foot in front of the other as given to do, staying where harmony is as much as possible you will be amazed at what comes into expression.

When you go to God all you are seeking is harmonious expression; harmony in all aspects, facets and pieces of your life working like a well oiled machine and it is! Your entire expression is a perfectly timed beautifully played piece of music where one thing comes in at the perfect time, fades off without notice as another bar is manifest into expression. The music flows through you to be experienced in the outer world and the perfection you felt when it was given to you is the perfection received when it is received by those receptive.

God **is** harmonious expression and once you begin to recognize what you are experiencing is harmonious living under grace you won't ever want to let it go because life gets no easier than when you let harmony be your expression because you realize there is no reason to struggle anymore because God's got it handled.

17.

Man is under natural law which apply to the behaviors of the human man whereas spiritual man is under the Law of One which is the unseen creative consciousness that is the allness and entirety of all that is defined as *this universe* including you as child of God.

18.

Normal and natural

Normal and natural for man is to be within their rights, legal and moral, to kill for self defense or imminent harm or for any reason the court of law and the court of man deem acceptable.

Normal and natural for spiritual man is harmonious, peaceful, quiet and without power therefore rests in the harmonious expression they are of. Whatever happens to spiritual man is because of who he is and it is never just for them personally but also for the good of all who desire that which is being offered-harmonious expression of being.

Depending on where you present from, man of earth or man of God, determines what is normal and natural and thereby shouts to the world the source of your consciousness.

19.

God **is** the good appearing as good in your experience, not God *sending good for* your experience. God is not separate and apart from all that is harmonious therefore you cannot have harmonious expression without knowing God aright because God **is** the harmony, the joy you express because it is how you feel.

God the source appears as God the effect. In thy presence is fullness, the allness of God, infinity. God declaring itself, God revealing itself as Self, God the Father revealing itself as God the son, you in expression when it is known.

20.

God doesn't *give* you anything God **is** everything and you are of God therefore you are sustained and maintained by that which you are of-God.

21.

God is harmony experienced. You feel light, life is easy, you are in a flow. When you experience *inharmony* it is because you are thinking and behaving as a human.

The feeling of anything other than harmony instantly reveals you are separated from God in consciousness and have slipped back into duality. What do you do? Take a breath, settle on a Truth, take it within and rest until you get the feeling, the knowing God is present, on the field then go back to what you were doing letting this state of consciousness be your consciousness out in the world.

This is how you get yourself out of the way and let God do what God does-perfect your world to its specification of harmony. God is the brains and you are consciousness in form for the work to be done.

22.

Spiritual man has no sanctimony/moral superiority because spiritual man has no desire to be known of man or the world.

23.

The more you develop your consciousness the more you lay the foundation for the next generation to develop theirs to even a greater degree which means more children will be born into spiritual households thus instead of these children having to unlearn human ways of being they are taught Truth from the very beginning **as their nature.** One child of spiritual nature in a school of a thousand would change the dynamics of those children.

Remember one with God is a majority because only one with God has reign/dominion over their experiences ie man of God determines their experience purely by their being in oneness with God. God being the only creative expression of which all is of, is both cause and effect. Therefore you always get that which is the allness of God because God is both cause and effect.

Those of you who want consistency in your life want God in your life. No surprises, no catches, no ifs, ands or buts. Straight up follow the rules-there is only one expression of good and we call it God, and that all are of the same source, this expression of good.

Man of earth however never knows minute to minute what is going to come across their path because they have no way of determining whether it is going to be a good day or a bad day. This duality of possibilities is the good and bad of man's existence and the cause of the chaos and sin in the world.

24.

You have to stop trying to *define* God in human terms; you cannot. However you can **experience** God and realize there is no defining God in human terms only the knowing of God through an experience where no definition is necessary.

25.

Man eternally seeks for what God gives freely.

26.

The only gratitude that is a healing agency is the gratitude for God, the gratitude for God realization of harmonious expression and abundance in any and all form from the smallest to the biggest because your oneness with the Father constitutes the allness of your supply.

Your gratitude is for the Truth that has made you free through study and practice and now you are in a position to bring that light to others just by thanking Father, being truly dumbfounded at times when "the stars literally line up" and your day is as if in a dream, so smooth, so perfect, so peaceful there was no other explanation than it was under grace, the allness of God in expression.

27.

Every time you have a conscious realization of the spirit within somebody in the outer world benefits by it. Now do you see why this light cannot be hidden? Cannot stay under a basket? Everyone who attains even a tiny measure of this Light is called upon to share it with the world because it is impossible not to share what you feel when it is bursting forth from you.

28.

Understand if you aspire to be a spiritual master you will be the servant of all who need anything on the face of the earth but also understand the help you will be asked for is merely the opening of your conscious oneness to allow harmony to be your expression to all those who desire the grace or presence of God.

Regardless of who you are, what your faith is, what your political association is, your gender, your personal habits, traits or origin, grace is the harmonious expression of God as your harmonious expression when it is known byway of an actual experience of the Father within.

The ground on which you stand is holy ground, the body is the temple of the consciousness within, the Christ consciousness, Father, God, harmonious expression expressing infinitely through you as you when you are in conscious oneness with it.

29.

You cannot be under grace if you are living under the law of man.

You cannot be under grace if you pick up the sword.

You cannot be under grace if you believe in good and evil.

You cannot be under grace if you fear anything.

To fear is to be an atheist for if you fear you do not know God aright.

You can only have grace/harmony when you give up the weapons and ways of the world and come to the understanding that **He hangeth the world on nothing.**

30.

Conscious oneness with God **is** the healing principle.

Conscious oneness reveals Truth.

Conscious oneness with God is your true nature.

You heal merely by knowing the nature of error as illusion, no thing.

You are a healing agent every moment you are with God.

Knowing the source of Truth brings Truth to bear, God on the field.

Communion, oneness heals all belief in a power separate and apart from God.

Knowing the Truth of error heals.

The result of nothingizing error is Truth revealed, God is and God is harmony in your midst.

Healing means bringing God to bear, grace in your midst to dispel the erroneous belief in anything other than good, harmony, peace.

Healing is grace, the allness of God in action in your experience.

Grace is the allness of God in action ie the good of God is your experience in all ways.

Being one with God is the healing principle. Why? Because when you bring Truth to your consciousness you bring Truth to bear out in the world among man where it wasn't before. You reveal Truth within yourself and this is the ripple, the wave that goes out from you to those in need **not** of *your* doing but of **God's** as and through you.

It may seem like I say the same thing over and over but it helps me order God's thoughts for the expulsion of the human belief when Truth comes into awareness. The "if this then that" until I get to that one sentence that brings the entire message into focus, codified and simple to understand. But you might grasp the meaning from any of the statements because we all interpret words and the way they are used differently according to where we are from and our history. I am redundant for cause-so that one of the similar but different explanations clicks in your consciousness as something you can get your teeth in, you get it and want to know more.

Understand when I am doing this process it *isn't me personally,* the me of man, thinking these thoughts it is God bringing Truth to me one baby step at a time on a logical level, the "if this then that," and then the big reveal happens, the Truth God was leading me toward understanding of comes into focus and wham! Revelation! Deep understanding in which I can release a belief because Truth has just been revealed.

When this happens my thinking mind willingly and happily lets go of belief because Truth feels stable, woosah, middle ground, peace, deep breath and sigh, you get it and now you can rest because Life makes that much more sense now with that revealed Truth tucked in your pocket.

31.

God within is the Truth of your being and this can only be understood byway of an actual experience of God within your own being. This experience reveals the Truth that **I am that I am,** the Father and I are one, I am the prodigal son returning home, I am the individualized expression of the one source of all that exists visible and invisible. This revealed in consciousness heals you, returns you to your true state of being as spirit and not human.

Healing understood mystically is that which restores man to his true nature, true expression of being as that of spirit in oneness with God. A healing reveals man's error of thinking and Truth restores man to his rightful place as son of God. You have always been a prince but have borne the weight of a pauper only to one day stumble on that which reveals your true nature, that of a prince, one of standing and bearing because of his **heritage.**

Does this pauper now knowing himself to be a prince continue to live the way he had been? Wouldn't he return to his Father whom he has never known but feels drawn to beyond reason? Would he expect anything other than welcoming arms from one who created him and seemingly lost him? Would you run or walk to this union of Father and son?

This is mankind with calloused hands and hardened hearts unaware of the stamp of prince across his forehead. If you but look within you will find the sign pointing to the Truth you unknowingly bear witness to- the Father within, harmony, love, peace, home.

32.

The words must go deeper than the thinking mind into that which is called the fertile soil, the receptivity within, the vacuum waiting to be filled with the allness that is the promise of God. You have to break through the mind to reach consciousness otherwise you are living by mere words, nothingness and are a husk, dry and empty of Truth, of Love, of eternal sustenance by which to be whole, ripe, full to overflowing.

There is an intuitive faculty and it works on two levels, on the cosmic level and on the spiritual level. The cosmic level is the level of man and man's intuitive faculties are nothing more than sense organs more attuned to sensation others may not be aware of. Man believes this to be the sixth sense, the one beyond the physical five of the human body and to a point it may be but **because the one with these psychic abilities still lives duality** their *gifts* are of duality therefore cannot be of any spiritual nature or expression of higher conscious knowing than man.

The spiritual level is not your senses relaying information rather it is being open and empty so God can be the Law unto your experience. With God at the helm of you you are under the Law of God which is harmony thus you don't need to *use* your intuitive faculties by which to navigate this world rather you **rest,** receive impartations and are always under the Law of grace, peace and harmony. God intuits for you what you are to rely on. God does the work; all you have to do is listen and respond, do and be in the harmony of God within.

33.

There are no tomorrows, there is only now therefore if God is active in your life now God will be active in all your nows. Those nows become the tomorrows of now. Therefore the reason to not hoard what is given but to give of it freely, not wastefully but in the knowing that what is now will forever be now if that is where you are. This is the infinity of expression.

34.

God is the atmosphere you exist in therefore experience.

35.

Government protects *their* interests over the good of the people they are charged with protecting against outside forces where by making those they are supposed to be protecting the price paid for *their* advancement.

Governmental power is predicated on the use of subversive psychological tactics for the sole purpose of enslaving citizens under the guise of protection and are the ones that are used to do the will of the current government. This has nothing to do with the needs of citizens crying out for basic human rights and dignities but *their* own greed, need of power or immoral proclivity.

All the governments of the world are just bigger Epstein islands because the result is the same-the demoralization, enslavement, rape and subjugation of the weak by the powerful for play.

God saves man through revelation of their true nature as child of God and rises you above the government of man predicated on fear, compliance and threat of death. In the face of any foreign power, **any power other than God,** of self or of the world, you who know your Truth can never again be a puppet of the world but always remember secret, silent and sacred because for this work to change the world it can only be shared by example, expression not words from the mouth speaking duality.

36.

Temporary loss leads to permanent glory.

37.

Human knowledge/academia blocks or inhibits spiritual growth because the intelligent mind will fight to keep its function as thinker because it knows stuff and must protect you from yourself. That knowing of stuff needs to be died to so you can be filled back up with Truth. Until you are willing to give up all you hold *as* Truth you will not find Truth.

The price to pay for Truth, God, is surrender, willing surrender for God to take back the direction of your Life by revealing your true nature to you so you become instrumental to your own transformation. You are your own salvation, or not, because in choosing God you are choosing eternal life which is the salvation of God. God is always a choice, yours.

38.

Religion isn't "I'm better than you" sanctimonious lip service, it is the realization of an inner peace and the desire to loose it for the individual salvation of man.

39.

Everything necessary for your experience always appears.

40.

You are to reveal to the world the kingdom of heaven here on earth through your oneness with God and the expression of God as you is the living Christ, Truth expressing, harmony in your midst.

41.

The activity of the Christ realized in individual consciousness is the Law unto every form of discord and the avenue of good unto your experience.

42.

How ripe are you?

Everyone is at a different stage of consciousness within stages of consciousness. There are those who are super ripe and instantly understand and crave more and more light while others are slower to comprehend. It has nothing to do with you, how smart you are, how hard you are trying. It has nothing to do with you rather it is the amount of humanhood embodied, relied upon, expressed that is keeping you from being open to Truth.

Those who are ripe have removed the obstacles from their mind and are desirous of what is not known, they want something to sink their teeth in and finally get understanding the world has not provided. One who isn't ripe may just be coming onto this path, stay a while, go back to duality, play around with some mind healing and then come back having learned a bit more to make them curious instead of just over the line of indifference.

States and stages my friend, this is a journey not a sprint.

43.

Spiritual instruction comes only in the deepest of humility which says "I am empty, I know nothing, Father fill me up!" And in that expression of self receive Self because there is readiness, hunger and need of what can be received-the things of God not man.

44.

Truth cannot be heard while you are thinking because Truth comes in the silence.

45.

I is the doer of you therefore your function is to listen and do as given. This is how spiritual man lives. You do what you are given to do when it is received, usually a small task that needs to be done so the rest can continue coming into expression and the rest of the time you are in a state of inner listening but you are just doing life as is normal and natural to you.

Living in God is not arduous, living as man is.

46.

There is only one gift of God and that is God itself as the allness unto your eternal existence.

47.

God is Life and this Life is Self sustained.

48.

That human man believes he is separated from God is the cause of all the error human man experiences.

49.

There is an infinite power of good where you are and it is universal intelligence, an all knowing consciousness awaiting your recognition to become active in your life.

50.

When your consciousness has become so imbued with the realization that the continuous activity of God within you is the true source of all supply you have reached the consciousness of one supported by grace in all ways for Truth in consciousness becomes bread on the water pressed down and flowing over-visible supply in your awareness.

Days 51-100

51.

Look through the appearance to the Truth behind the appearance so that as quickly as possible you recognize that it is not a power facing you but merely remnants of a universal belief in that which is unlike the harmony of God with no Law, Substance or objectivity thus unreal.

52.

Your past has no power unless you give it permission. Nothing that concerns the past has to do with you who is living in the now.

53.

Subject yourself to God's impartations which are not man's thoughts and you are subject only to the cause and effect of God which is good.

54.

Are they your fears or the world's fears upon you? Go to God and ask for its Truth of your sense impression, never use your own as that is what keeps the atmosphere of man thick, heavy and suffocating.

55.

God is not where God is not known in awareness.

56.

Father show me the path I am to follow today. I don't need to know about tomorrow for there is no tomorrow, only a continuation of now. I need not know anymore than what you need me to know now for I know in the next now you will continue to impart to me what it is I am to do and be and will never stop for in the now is where you exist therefore it must be where I exist.

57.

Leave people be out in the world, do not correct or intrude rather go within to release grace and bless those in the outer world that they might find Truth.

58.

God feels the purity of your motive, intention with every breath you take; God will not be mocked, cheated, used or tricked. It isn't your words alone that keep you in the kingdom, **it is your motivation for being in the kingdom that God responds to**-that you desire only God.

59.

There is always God so there is always a solution, not a human one but a spiritual one and it will be given from within for you to express.

60.

Step to the side and let God go first in all ways.

61.

Your dependence on the Father for all things is what takes you out of the materialistic sense of the world where man is dependent on man and the things of man and this alone is the key.

To chose to be dependent on God, the invisible within, you are admitting the world of man has nothing left to offer you and that the only reality is in the invisible.

There is no thing called material or matter there is only spirit in form. What man exchanges and depends on is material, but material isn't anything but a concept for what is visible, tangible and measurable but has no Truth, reality of expression.

The things of God are permanent, inexhaustible and infinite. That which comes from God byway of bread on the water you cast returned upon you is yours for as long as you have need of it. When you have no need you pass it on for another to benefit by and it is still permanent in its existence until or if the person in possession of it *uses it for the ways of man, for evil, control, pride, ego.*

In that moment what was a gift of God for the good of all becomes duality in expression. All that is from God is for good regardless of what it is. It is man who in their hypnotism takes that which is good and uses it in some way to benefit self or against another physically or mentally and the harmony of singularity is lost until it is once again realized in consciousness as neither good or bad but **is**.

62.

The peace within creates the peace without

The peace within appears as the manna without

I will never leave you nor forsake you but **you must abide in Me,** by every Word that comes out of My mouth which is your mouth when you are in conscious oneness with God.

63.

As you go about your daily living let your expression be "my peace I give unto you, not as the world gives it to you but My peace, the Christ peace I give unto you."

Your function is to be a benediction, a blessing so that wherever you go you can bestow God's grace on those still in darkness/ignorance.

64.

Grace maintains, sustains and governs all who enter into My consciousness.

65.

Always remember good can become bad and bad can become good. Therein lies the pain of living as a human-always striving to hold onto the little good you glean in the face of evil but if you live **is** there is no opposite therefore what **is** is eternally good/God in expression.

66.

Life is perspective which comes from conscious understanding of the nature you think yourself to be. If you think you are man you are living out from the nature of man which is the universal belief in duality but if you know God by way of experience you are living your nature as God expressing which is good, harmony.

67.

Seek God for peace and not purpose (things, desires, reason) and in the peace shall come all that is needed for a bountiful life.

68.

"What say ye Father?" Is the abracadabra of the spiritual Life. It is you asking for communication, for Truth from Source. You have come a long way when you no longer look to yourself for answers but go to God. This is walking the path aright, this is the way Life is done with God in your midst and this is living heaven on earth in oneness with the Father.

69.

When you know your true identity you have no more demonstrations to make. Why? There is nothing left for you to pray for because you have come to the realization all needs are met through the relationship of oneness.

70.

God is my good. God is the health of my countenance, safety and security, my high tower, my rock, my foundation. God is my abiding place, my home. I live and have my being in the secret place of the most High hidden away from the world. My body maybe seen but not the I of my being because I live in an inner awareness of God. My body is out there walking and working in the world but I am not. I am living in the temple that is within me, the temple that is my consciousness and this consciousness takes form in the outer world as the needed and the added things.

71.

God is the only power but not a power to be used. The power of God is in the consistent reliability of God in your awareness that is ever present to help you to navigate this life from a higher state of knowing therefore expression.

72.

Stop resisting evil. Evil does not exist. What does exist is a *false belief* in that which is unlike God, that of good and evil. When you lose that belief you understand evil is no thing more than personal perspective expressing.

73.

Acknowledge God in all expressions and the easiest way to do this is to know **God is as all** and in that way do not malpractice yourself by still thinking matter and material are real. Only God is real and God is as all. God is the sufficiency unto your existence as the provisions needed.

When you have God you have all there is therefore all you will ever want.

74.

The desire to know and learn can only come from within a person, not by the desire of one *for* another. Secret, silent and sacred. You do not give pearls to swine, a person not ready for this knowledge, for it would be as useless to them as pearls would be to a pig.

Nothing you do will bring another any closer to finding Truth, the God within *except* prayer, silent listening for God's Truth to shatter belief thereby freeing those receptive that much more from the errors of man.

75.

The Presence announces itself byway of fruitage experienced.

76.

Only those of spiritual vision can behold a spiritual demonstration of the presence of God which is the only demonstration spiritual man can make because when you demonstrate the presence of God you have manifested the allness of God as the added things.

77.

That which I am seeking I am.

What do you seek? Truth. I am Truth. Immortality? I am immortality. Eternality? I am eternality. Peace? Abundance? I am all those things and more but you must give up your life-your desires, your hates, your fears and your loves and **let** God fill you with that which you are supposed to express defined by the all knowing God and not your finite sense of human good.

The thing about God is that there are no strings attached to the good you receive and you get used to receiving good. Human man doesn't trust good and waits for the other shoe to drop because no thing in man's experience is permanent rather must be constantly adjusted to balance the every shifting expression of duality.

78.

As you come to know God you begin to desire less from the outer world and as you desire less and less from the world and rest in oneness with God you become **desire-less.** You come to realize the world holds no thing for you and that God holds all you desire and you already have God within you so in this way you become desire-less because there is no thing to desire when you are the beholder of all that **is** already yours.

Now do you see how a spiritual man will never be seen lacking? Begging bread? Because they know there is no thing they are not able to receive because all is already within and God knows your needs before you do.

The life of God is all about trust. I know that word is a hard one for most people because there has not been one single person you have been able to trust implicitly. But you can trust God. But if you trust God you **trust** God. I have the word *Relinquish* tattooed on my arm. I put it there almost 20 years ago when I was trying to find God. One thing I knew without a doubt, but often forgot hence the tattoo as a visual reminder, was if I ask God for his way be done I had to step back and let his way be done instead of thinking about it, doing something to help the process along. I thought of prayer as a balloon with a string and I was offering it up to God but in order for it to be in his hands and his hands alone I had to let go of the string. I had to **relinquish** the desire to control that which I asked God to do.

Obviously I too was of the God outside of me version but beyond this error I was learning to defer as I asked for his will to be done. This is the very nature of spiritual man. When you heal an error you have to let it go because you just proved to yourself error isn't if God is. If you continue to think of the error, chew on it like stale gum ruminating and thinking *what if's* you are keeping yourself from hearing the voice of God because it is so noisy up in there!

See it. Know it. Relinquish it

Error presents. Error is an illusion. Let it go for it is no thing.

79.

Do not get discouraged! For most of us it is a long period of wrong directions, corrections, finding modalities that fit our conscious understanding at the moment and then as consciousness opens so does your understanding of how all of this plays out. Then one day it clicks. All of it up unto this point, all the mishmash of information falls into line, orders itself and presents itself to you as the perfect gift of understanding. In that moment *the light shines where there was darkness, now you see*. You can then look out and no longer see a world that needs to be healed, changed or reformed. You now see God's love beginning to blossom breaking the mesmerism of humanhood.

80.

Freedom in God:

Whenever you are going through a period of illness, unhappiness, lack of peace, prosperity or frustration remember that **this has nothing to do with your outer world.** You will be tempted to believe that the external world is causing the difficulty, but this is not so. If you can discern that this represents a battle going on *within yourself* you will quickly achieve victory just through the ability to discern that no person, condition or situation is doing anything *to* you. This is a battle within you in which your higher Self is seeking ascendency over the mortal/material/carnal sense into which you were born. This is the son of God in you struggling to come into expression.

You do not seek victory over outer conditions or person, rather let the Christ of you come into ascendancy and it will be the light revealing that there is no darkness.

Every moment of every day man fights man for things man cannot give man and what man is truly looking for is the ascendency of their higher Self, for freedom, to not live as animals but to live a life of harmony with supply, good will and joy but man has no idea that is what they are seeking because the material world says there is only material things to seek to fill the void within.

But what man seeks is freedom by way of knowing God and that can only be attained individually. Freedom is not collective, it is individual for no man can free another, only you can free you.

Man does not realize it is freedom they seek and it is only found through God, the higher Self of being. Man unknowingly seeks a *thing* to fill the emptiness but because man has no idea what they are seeking to fill the emptiness **is** Truth **man associates the feeling of emptiness as lack of outer things, dissatisfaction** and thus perpetuates the horrors of man trying to create a life for themselves separate and apart from their true spiritual nature which does and will fill all the emptiness within.

No matter the names man gives to express his present conditions of lack they all stem from one thing: believing they are separated from God, Source. All it takes is realizing you are **of** God and this Truth will make it possible for you to free yourself from the weight of the world for God is the state of consciousness where there is no weight to bear for what you thought was reality has been shown to be nothingness and in that light there is no dark because ignorance has been dispelled.

81.

You cannot use spiritual power because there is none to be used. Spiritual power is recognition of oneness and oneness is your protection, your supply, your life and your heritage.

82.

Beholding is a quiet process of observance, not an active process of the mind where the mind searches for something to do. This is the difference between spiritual man and mortal man.

In spiritual living you do not use the mind as a problem solver by reaching out/taking thought to get God to do something rather settle down and let consciousness behold. This is the attitude used in healing. When someone asks for help instead of the mind of the healer reaching out for some human fix he settles back so he can behold God in his consciousness knowing all error no matter name or nature is illusion, of duality, and as such are treated the same-as no thing in the presence of one power, God on the field the appearance dissolves.

No matter what you are doing you are never looking at people as male or female, rich or poor, sick or well. The ordinary person looks and sees man and woman but that is not the Truth of being therefore after a time of practice you will see God behind the person in essence, that being their true identity and not what you are presented with in the visible world.

As a healer or teacher you cannot afford to see students or patients as attractive, ugly or anywhere in between. **You train yourself so your attention is on the listening within** and not the seeing without because regardless of the claim someone brings to you or you are presented with personally **the answer is always the same**-there is no claim, it is illusion because if you have an awareness of God within, have communion, communication, a relationship with God, you can rest knowing this is the only reality, the only Truth unto your being.

83.

It is only in the degree that you continue your humanness that you miss the full attainment of spiritual harmony.

84.

You can only heal someone of their human beliefs by beholding the Christ of them and in this way reveal the Christ as the reality of their being.

But understand grace, the peace and harmony of God unto your Life is a constant dispensation **only when there is union with God** therefore when you go to a healer you will receive some form of relief but there is always that warning **to go and sin no more lest a worse fate befall you.** This means if you are going to continue living in duality you will continue to suffer duality in greater and greater degree until you decide to turn from the world and live with God. I mean why not? If you are going to take a bite/get a healing and know that it is great, why not buy the whole meal/get oneness with God?

Yes, there are things you are afraid of having to give up but have you thought of **what will you gain?** Ponder that, go within, ask the big guy why he loves you so much, ask for his presence and you will see why you will love him so much. Ps. Bring tissue, you will need tissue.

85.

Sin and error:

You are not your sins, you are released from your sins and fears when you know these are not *of you* but are of an impersonal belief held by the world-a belief in a power separate from the good of God.

Think of sins as spots of mud on your being. They are *on* you, not *of* you therefore they can be wiped away. Though your sins be scarlet, the dirt, you are white as snow-true spiritual nature-that is too pure to behold inequity ie more than one power or an opposing expression of harmony.

If you hold everyone in this light that you yourself just bathed in there are no sinners, no irredeemable souls for nothing tarnishes the soul and you must see that though appearances may bring judgement from man, one of spiritual illumination sees past illusions/judgements to the Christ within **and that is how you begin to forgive yourself, your neighbor, your enemy and bring God onto the field to awaken those who are lost in this world.**

The sin is the belief in duality as reality of man's expression.

The correction of the sin is the knowing of God by actual experience.

86.

You cannot reach the realm of God except through silence.

87.

Divine consciousness is released *through* an individual and permeates their atmosphere like the sweetest perfume but unlike perfume it never leaves because it cannot be withdrawn. This is spiritual perfume and once it is released it remains and those with awareness of discernment feel it. That is why holy places *feel* different; it feels as if you are being enveloped in a different atmosphere, it is tangible and your Christ responds ie goosebumps, flush, warmth, a presence wrapped around you. It is peace, calm, a place to rest, cry, let go and rise again knowing you are supernaturally supported by this feeling which is the grace of God, the all of God, spiritual perfume of forgiveness and wholeness.

88.

The spiritual things of God are not understood by mortal man therefore when you speak of God you can only speak it **to** God, that being the Self of you. You cannot talk about this to human man or you lose your demonstration. What does to lose your demonstration mean? It means that you are using your humanness, ego, words, to introduce God to someone instead of letting the Christ of you awaken the Christ within them by **your** expression which speaks volumes as to who you are.

You will have more spiritual experiences than you have ever had in your life. If you have had none, you should begin to have them because all your work now is at that stage of receiving spiritual blessings. **Keep the experiences secret and sacred, close to your heart, unspoken of, and they will multiply.** Let them bear fruit and when the fruit is visible, has been experienced as Truth by you, then and only then can you share with those who ask in earnest to know what you know.

What can be given to one who seeks is a measure commensurate with the degree of **their receptivity** ie consciousness. Therefore what is given beyond silent prayer is milk for those dipping in to see what spirituality is and meat for those starving for what you know.

89.

You can only teach what you know and what you know is completely dependent on your degree of living the **nature** of God in expression which is harmony.

90.

The learning of spiritual principles *educates the human mind out of itself* as you learn the Truth about your spiritual nature. You are able to feel Truth more often as the unseen world begins to unfold as your reality and more confirmation that the world of man *is* the dream, the false reality of duality. You are not forcing yourself to try to believe something isn't when it is rather you are able to let go of old human beliefs because Truth of God has brought light to the error expressing.

We are getting the human mind to give up its reliance on its own powers of judgement, good and evil, money, princes and powers which allows for more and more conscious realization that **there is no God power to do anything to evil.** That cannot be taught by one who has **not** had the mystical experience of oneness.

You must have had the experience of God to teach of the mystical experience otherwise it is nothing more than human philosophy on a hypothetical level of understanding which is back in the realm of duality.

91.

You cannot feel spiritual, you can only be spiritual, it isn't a feeling it is a being. You do not *feel* your nature, you **express** your nature.

92.

Praying, inner listening for Truth attunes you to the consciousness by which you can receive Truth.

93.

The easiest way to serve God is to recognize the God of man and not the outward expression of man and in this way greet all as brothers in Christ regardless of outward appearance. This is the hallmark of spiritual man for only spiritual man knows the Truth of human man as child of God, brother of my brother, pea of God's pod.

94.

Living out from the nature of God becomes the Law of harmony unto your Life ie your being, health, supply because God is these things in expression as you.

95.

Your security is in your union with God, oneness of being, whole and complete never to part.

96.

For those not ready these words and this study isn't clear and it isn't doable. This is not to say you won't be ready and yes, it does get infinitely clearer.

This is a **process** of letting go of cherished biases, hates, judgements, grudges and desires you have been accumulating, housing, feeding that have become the way you view the world and yourself and/or how you *feel* the world has labeled you. So yes, this can be uncomfortable at times because we like our stuff, it makes us feel safe. Without our stuff we are naked, weapon-less, powerless against the forces of man and the world.

Yes! That is exactly where you want to be but with one little tweak that makes all the difference to your eternal Life: You may have no weapons of man on which to depend but what of it? What does it matter you have no weapons when **your** Father goes before you to make the crooked places straight? Makes your atmosphere the presence of peace?

What weapon would you need in the presence of peace? None for God is your protection from needing weapons because there is no need of protection when your expression is good as is the intent of the expression.

Do you see why spiritual man does not need weapons on which to stand? Because the only ones who need weapons are the ones who fear the weapons of man. Spiritual man cannot die therefore has no fear of what man can do to him thus needs no weapons to protect life or limb. God goes before you to make the crooked places straight, harmony on your path, but only if you are in conscious union with God as your Life, your every day livingness, expression, who you are and not what you turn to now and again for purpose. You do not use God rather you desire God and all you want is given without asking.

This process is simple in theory, harder in reality but doable! No pressure! God's pace, not yours. Believe me, I have had a few conversations about its time vs. my time and I can tell you with egg on my face I always see the error of my thinking. Ahhh. Did you see that? My thinking. I take my own foot and bash myself over the head with it. God didn't do a damn thing but shake his head like a true Father saying "seriously? We are doing this again? Ok, give me a few, I need popcorn for this."

You are never alone and there is never a reason to be afraid or fear you aren't getting it. Just sit, lay, walk or run but open yourself up to God and it will tell you the most freaking awesome stuff ever! You go Prince of Peace!

97.

There is only ever one place you are expected to be and that is in the consciousness of God-communing, communicating, having a relationship, learning, practicing, healing, and expressing. It becomes automatic and you won't hardly think about the process at all after a while as you become fluent, in the flow of what was before steps and stages.

It is akin to breathing-you do it, it just is and it is only when you have stopped breathing for whatever reason, by holding it or otherwise, do you become aware something has changed.

In spiritual sense what you become aware of is being human ie emotional, edgy, thinking or wallowing in the past or worrying about some aspect of the future. What you are feeling is duality, the life you used to experience. Basically you have wandered out of God consciousness back into duality and this shift in how you feel within is the indication something is off.

Where you were was peaceful, it was more and more your normal expression. The only reason you are able to realize something is different is because you have slipped back into **who you used to express as, duality,** and it has become a foreign feeling because it isn't your normal expression anymore.

The solution to being back where peace is is simple. You already recognized you were out of the flow of God so you take a breath, shake it off with a little chuckle and go within to feel God's sunny vibe on your face, feel that smile coming back and feel your shoulders drop. "I got this," you hear within and you smile, your invisible partner is on the scene once again able to make the crooked places straight.

We all fall out of synch. The measure of your desire to live the harmony and peace God provides is how fast you get back in synch with God and the lessening frequency of falling out of God consciousness.

98.

In the degree that you are able to receive impartations of spirit the mind doesn't function at all except on the human level of awareness, memory or cognitive ability and find you require less and less reasoning ability because you have more and more access to God's impartations.

Where before you would have had to think or reason now seems almost automatic. You become aware of answers without any thinking or reasoning process but it isn't *you*, it is **God** imparting the information **to** you and you are doing the physical work in a world of visible forms.

I can attest to this a hundred times over. I will be in a conversation that seems to turn to an area I am not familiar with and all of a sudden my mouth opens and the correct place, answer, idea or solution comes tumbling out. I seriously feel as if sometimes I get hijacked but in a good way. So as the words are coming out of my mouth my brain is going what? Seriously? Oh crap, did I just spew like a know-it-all on a soap box? Ready to retract I suck in my breath and then someone says "perfect! That sounds really good, thanks that just gave me an idea, yes, that is the name I just couldn't pull it out." And then I let out my breath silently and smile over the funny mouth shape. God says "no one noticed."

99.

Your mental image of those you know are nothing like who they really **are.** Would I know myself by your description? Highly unlikely for your description of me is solely based on whether you see me as a human or as a brother. If you see me as a human your perception of me is all over the map, changeable one day to the next but if you see me through the eyes of the Father you are seeing another exactly like yourself-individualized spirit.

100.

This earth is filled with the voice of God when material thought is stilled.

Days 101-150

101.

The only disease man has is material sense/duality. If you feel like life is a ping pong ball tournament being played in your living room you are living as man and are not of the conscious awareness of God.

102.

Seek God and all will be given unto you for

God is your peace

God is your security

God is your Life

God is your eternality

God is your expression of God in form

God is your supply

God is your release from pain/disease

God is your companionship

God is your resting place

God is all there is and you are of God. All you need to do is seek God. Where do you seek God? In the quiet when the mind is still. This presence is omnipotent, omniscient and omnipresent. There is no thing you need rather you just don't know what or where your allness is and that is the entire purpose of this writing, to teach you how to become aware of and live with God, Father, the One, the Comforter.

Do not be the one who makes excuses for not following your heart because though there will be many more chances, why live in this world of duality when you can live heaven on earth and enjoy, rejoice at the life you will begin to live?

Find God and the pain stops

Find God and the supply flows

Find God and friends appear

Find God and your relationships change

Find God and peace, safety and security come.

Take your present circumstance and turn it into an opportunity to realize God and begin your journey home.

103.

How can you pray that one be safe and in the same breath pray another dies? You cannot pray duality, you cannot pray to use God to do what you desire or think necessary or just. You know nothing but what God reveals as Truth and in that Truth you are brought back to the Truth that **all the error that exists in your world is of your own creation out of the belief in more than one power** and thus have separated yourself from the consciousness of God which is separating yourself from your peace.

104.

You can only save yourself if you pray for your enemy.

You can't save your life at the expense of another; you can only save your life by giving your life for another and this isn't done blindly, it is done through knowing your Truth that you are eternal and immortal as God. One who knows their true nature would not fear death knowing the end of this form functioning is just the end of this form functioning and nothing more nor less.

105.

Anything less than God's perfection is illusion.

106.

You have no qualities, the body has no qualities, all qualities belong to God and flow from you **as** your qualities to the world. Therefore when you encounter others who are not giving forth the qualities of God at the moment know that whatever they are showing of a negative nature aren't *their* qualities per se but the duality of the world, the atmosphere, the carnality, the materialism that is coming from them. Neither human man nor spiritual man have qualities unto themself rather express the consciousness formed of the atmosphere they marinate in.

107.

All of us have our Achilles heel when it comes to man's inhumanity. For me it is animals and of course every story about an animal being abused just tears at my heart. Yes I know Truth but that doesn't erase the ache in my soul for any innocent.

I came across a story that took me to my knees with rage. I mean rage like I had never felt before, I was literally shaking and wanted to run and not stop. My heart broke at the sight of this dog even though it was a happy ending. I asked God to help me understand my rage at the perpetrators and just like that comfort came.

What did that person endure as a child? What duality ie pain, suffering both physical and mental, did that innocent child experience that would express as a personality lacking empathy? What could have been done that created the notion of maiming for sport? What had that child endured that could cause such a disregard for life, a total lack of empathy and basic dignity of a living creature? It was at that moment I realized though that dog had suffered, and I'm sure many of this person's other victims did perish, they only suffered once, only died once.

That child most likely saw and experienced things most of us won't experience even once, day in and day out. The child made to hurt an animal or be hurt themselves, the child made to normalize pain and suffering, the child made to go within themselves to not be a part of what is being done to them. All of what the world threw at them stuck and created that expression man calls conscious-less or evil/bad.

I bring this up because what is seen in the world as atrocities are the extreme effects of duality upon a person/families/groups. When we see man's atrocities, the effect of their expression, we never stop to understand why, the cause which now you understand to be duality, the atmosphere of man with no God known in the picture.

There is no love in that child **because there was no God known within the parents to give of.** There was no God of Truth known within the parents, not even moral culpability/social norms by which to mitigate the effects of the world on themselves and their children.

Not until our children are protected from duality, protected from the errors of their parents and the conditions of loveless upbringings will the offenses against all living things stop. It is for this reason we share grace, bring God to bear to bring an opening for the light to shine through for one in need to glimpse, feel and chose to learn more.

108.

No thing can change man except a change in consciousness byway of something new being brought into awareness by experience.

This is why jails and forced rehabilitation will never work-it is a change of address, not a change in consciousness. There will always be jails but the goal through spiritual living is the silent sharing of divine love with the world, the kind word that keeps a person from doing self harm, the helping hand that changed the direction of another's life, being in the right place at the right time, being the expression of love someone needed to experience. It will take time to change the hearts and minds of man so until the time we are all of higher understanding there are certain moral conditions that will always be present-laws and enforcement of those laws.

The result of more God in awareness in the world is the lessening of the need for these moral corrections because fewer and fewer people are of the consciousness which facilitate their need.

109.

There aren't two of you, a real you and an unreal you, an unreal or real universe. There is only one you and only one universe-God's. But the minute you know good and evil you are kicked right out of Eden because you are then the man or woman of flesh that cannot please God and is not under the law of God because you wish to know *knowledge of good and evil.*

The cause of the entire fall of man, man separated from God in consciousness, is the word **knowledge.** *The finite knowing of man accumulated and passed down as Truth which is the definition of duality.* Once man desired what was **not** of God he lost the consciousness of God because he desired that which was **not of** the consciousness of God-the *knowing* of man.

God knows no such thing as human man because the very definition of *human* man is that of spiritual man separated from God no longer knowing its true nature, thus the reason human man is born and will die.

110.

God in the midst of you is the multiplier of loaves and fishes.

111.

You are immortal being and as such know you have nothing to fear because you are within God's grace/embrace. But when temptations come from the *snake,* the good and evil of man, remember this is where fortitude comes in, this is where spiritual integrity comes in, this is where the will of God comes in to be able to stand ye fast and ask yourself **will you ever again accept good and evil? Will you ever again accept** appearances at face value? Your answer should be a resounding **no**. Shake it off, say thank you to the Father and go on your way. You got this!

112.

Do not call a man stealing a thief. Be very careful of your reflexive responses to good and evil. Always remember you are not your sins, you are white as snow but though I, God, do not condemn thee, go and sin no more lest a worse fate befall you.

You are never held in judgement by God but you can hold yourself and others in **unrighteous** judgment which is the defining quality of man-judgement which in and of itself is based on personal beliefs and not Law. Spiritual man knows no labels, only Truth.

113.

If you can see it, hear it, taste it, touch it or smell it it isn't Truth, God, spirit rather it is a mental concept of the man of flesh who does not know God. It is only when you withdraw your estimate of what you *perceive* with the 5 senses that you realize it is neither good nor bad then are you at the beginning of a Life of wisdom, higher knowing beyond the thinking mind.

This life becomes a service to your fellow man because never can you serve your fellow man to the fullest while you are indulging in human good or human evil because inherent in that is judgement which will determine who you will serve and who you will not. Spiritual man serves all because all are you before you lost your ignorance of being.

114.

Human good is good as far as it goes but the salvation of mankind is not in good human men and women nor is it in men who can win wars. **The salvation of the world is upon those who correctly understand the first and second chapters of Genesis and the Sermon on the Mount.**

As long as you **are of the mind to use force against another** if necessary-mental, verbal or physical-you are the man of flesh, you are that Adam and that Eve that left the garden, the kingdom, the consciousness of God, to live in the environment of good and evil thus became subject to chance, outside forces and fears, accident, limitation, old age and death.

However if you put up the sword, give up the ways and means of human man to live under grace with God leading the way there is never a reason to use force because God reveals the non power of what man fights *believed* to be power.

115.

Withdraw all judgments and assessments of good and evil. It is difficult at first because in a way you have to live a dual life until this new way of being becomes more automatic, more in the consciousness of God than not. Then you hit the sweet spot where you are more often than not just being *of* this nature because of what it provides you.

116.

In the beginning of this journey you may feel fake, like you are trying to be that which you are not but you have to understand you have lived your whole life being fake, not experiencing life the way you should be so no, the spiritual path is not making a fake you, **it is revealing the real you** under the fake you you have been living as. You are revealing your Truth!

You are like an actor at this point, you are living a spiritual existence within consciousness but living outwardly as Joe next door who is super nice, always easy going, generous and seems to be doing pretty well for his or her self. No one but your spiritual peers know the source of all that is seen as success and happiness by man of earth nor would they understand it so you are outwardly Joe but inwardly spirit.

This isn't being fake, it is not making people uncomfortable by being all holy roller evangelical and losing your demonstration in the process by being sanctimonious instead of silent. You are silent about God through the lips while giving of grace through expression because that is how we roll.

117.

To forgive yourself or another is to be set free because you cannot ever be free if you hold another in bondage. However, there may be those things that just cannot be forgiven by you/man and that is ok. Give it to God. Be honest, say "I can't forgive them but I know you can." Turn to the Father and say "I can't find it in my heart to forgive them but you do it for me. I will turn the whole thing over to you to handle it."

If you hand it over you have to let it go completely. I tattooed the word relinquish on my arm because in my early days of praying to the old God outside of me I would *send up* a prayer envisioned as a balloon but I had to visualize myself letting go of the balloon string and let it float away completely. I had to completely relinquish ownership of that *balloon* by letting it go.

It is the same way with God. If you ask him, as in this instance of forgiveness, to forgive another you do not think about that person/situation again because you know by giving it to God it is being taken care of/worked out in a way far beyond your expectations or ability to bring about on your own.

You have to truly let go to receive grace for in the letting go you are trusting God, knowing without hesitation that God's got it and in this freedom of being there is no fret, worry, cogitating, or playing out the scenario over and over again. If it pops in, kick it in the butt; you are handled already, you are old news, nothing more than an echo.

118.

You have to desire peace over the chaos of man's drama if you ever want to know God aright.

119.

All that is necessary to this life you can receive from God, you don't need man for anything. All you need to do is turn within and feel that moment of inner peace and whatever is necessary for your life will come forth.

120.

You aren't getting humanly better, that isn't what God does. You are rising in consciousness *out of the humanhood* you have believed to be Truth all your life and are returning to your nature of spirit leaving the *concept* of man, body and death behind. You are not changing bad into good you are learning to live above opposites in oneness, wholeness, desireless-ness because God is all so what is there to desire once you find God?

121.

There is no i of you, there is only I, the Father within expressing as you to the visible world and this is the reason for the harmony you experience.

122.

If you are pretending to live by Truth because you think you will gain something over mortal man you will not because you are mortal man *pretending* to know God and all that will bring is human karma returned upon you. You are either working toward God, the promise of God, of kingdom and heaven of God or you are not. There is no grey area for God knows only **light, illumined consciousness,** and there is no distinction of consciousness or lesser consciousness. Consciousness of God is consciousness of God; anything else is human darkness/duality. One is reality and one is ignorance.

123.

You cannot hear the voice of God to guide, help and comfort you if your mind is chaotic, thinking of the past or the future. You have to be present, in the moment, **now,** to hear God and to hear God is to have your life ordered in a way that is harmonious, free flowing and almost effortless **because you are allowing God to flow and do and be for and as you.** Let God live your life and pay attention to the wonders you experience. That which has never caught your attention may do so now and the significance of it will bring tears to your eyes because now you see with the eyes of the Father.

124.

Living good and evil **traps you in good and evil** and only the ability to abide in God, in the realization no thing is good or evil is what frees you to live your Truth, oneness with the Father within.

125.

The secret of Life: there is no good nor evil. Don't try to tell this to anyone because they will laugh at you. But those of your consciousness will understand it and will have seen the fruitage of it ie when you are not judging by appearance good or bad you are living by grace. If you express the consciousness of God you will experience what the Bible calls *signs following*.

You must first be **of the consciousness** of God to be within the realm or Law of God and then all that is of God is available to you by way of your conscious connection to God. When you have this connection, signs follow; the things of God, of good, start to become evident in your life.

126.

Put your faith only in God realized, Truth revealed from within, and not in or on teachers, books or priests for though all may contain Truth, Truth can only be known as Truth from the Father when you ask for Truth to be known. What is received in consciousness may be the exact Truth you took in for understanding or it may be different but Truth unto you no less.

What has been received is now your Truth, the Truth you keep silent, secret and sacred while it grows within you until it is brought into outer expression as reality, Truth unto your being. Now you can share this Truth with the world silently or as meat for those already on the spiritual path because it is Truth unto you, **has become a demonstrated reality of your relationship with God.**

127.

God doesn't *do* anything. God **is** and God **is** Law. Law **is** and always **is** and never varies. Law is not personal, Law is universal so it isn't that God is doing anything **for** you it is that you are with God in consciousness and thus are within, **of** the Law that is the all of expression, God, a closed system beholden only to itself.

128.

Truth is not learned, Truth is revealed.

Only one thing can be known about God: God Is. Universal intelligence Is. Only God is and you are of is.

129.

No one can tell you what God is or is not. God reveals to you through study, application and communion what God is to you because God is an experience and it is individual.

130.

Nanuk: all we can know of God is that God is and anyone who thinks he *knows* God knows but a concept, an opinion, a belief about God.

Because to know God aright is an experience that changes your conscious understanding of reality.

131.

Come daily to that place of self examination where you realize this: there are a few fundamental principles that constitute the letter of Truth and they must never be forgotten because of their basic nature and because of the effect they have in your life.

God is as all-God is Spirit in nature and is the all of Life, one Law, Substance, Cause, Presence, Power. In other words to accept God as all means to accept God as constituting the allness of existence because God **is** eternal, Self maintaining and Self sustaining harmony without doing anything other than being where it **is**-consciousness.

132.

In the consciousness of **is** there is nothing to think about, mull over or chew on for is **is.** How do you keep chewing on something that **is?** you can't, is **is,** end of discussion and this is exactly where you are supposed to be in consciousness.

133.

It is in this continuous flow of being, is-ing that you are able to release, give away, share what you have because you know without a doubt new manna flows each day in conscious understanding and supply so those of Christ consciousness never feel the need to hoard, stash, covet or protect because nothing you release is lost, in fact to bless another with the use of it just brings more grace flowing through you and back to you for this is the Law of God. The more you release of God to the world through you being in conscious connection with God the more you experience what God created for you in the beginning for your experience.

Therefore to be and experience all you were created to be you must be **of** all that was created to be experienced and that is done by knowing your Truth by which your Truth can express.

134.

When you go to bed the only thought you are to carry into sleep is the Word of God, not the duality of man. Your last thoughts should be to ask God to keep your consciousness open so its work may go on while you sleep and that way your tomorrow begins in the awareness of God upon waking. "Good morning Father! Did I have a good night lol?! What lovely things are we going to do today?"

The only life you will ever live is the life you are living now because for future nows to be different you must consciously change in this now for it to be reflected as your Truth at a later **now**. Everything is chance if you don't chose better **now,** chose higher **now**, chose to know more **now** and begin to do **now** what is necessary for future **nows** to be of higher conscious understanding to live that expression of higher conscious understanding.

To have a different **now** you study and practice living Truth now and your future nows are a reflection of your now higher conscious understanding.

It will become automatic so don't stress. Just being with God tells God of your desire and that is all the opening God needs to start living your Life which changes your nows through evolution, systematic change due to a change in conscious understanding. You understand that God is what you are of and want to be with God therefore you evolve, grow, learn and become that which you desire to become.

Wishing, dreaming and thinking of how great it will be when it happens is going to remain wishing, dreaming and thinking **because change is conscious choice,** giving conscious consent and taking conscious action. Not *physical* action but **conscious** action of living with God. Wishing, dreaming and thinking are future tense and there is no future in God's expression, only evolving nows therefore the wish, dream or thought is the literal carrot on a stick six feet in front of your face you will never ever get because you are focused on the effect and not the cause of Life.

Evolution is the definition of raised consciousness thus man who raises his consciousness has evolved from the belief in being mortal to knowing their Truth as spirit in form, child of God.

135.

The exterminator of evil is the knowing of man's true nature. There is no great power coming to earth to destroy evil, the power to negate evil is already here and it is the knowing that there **is no good and no evil, only is.**

Remember your consciousness, each one of you, imbued with Truth, not good or evil, becomes the Law of resurrection, renewal, regeneration and restoration unto your existence. Your consciousness imbued with Truth becomes the Truth unto your experience, your personal experience living with God as your consciousness, your guide, direction, the all of you.

136.

The Word, God consciousness, becomes flesh means consciousness must take form out in the world for the good of all mankind. Spiritual wisdom is experiential, must be tangible, objective, it must bear fruit in your earthly experience but it cannot if you don't become consciously aware of it.

There is an infinity of Truth yet to be brought into man's knowing but it will remain in the invisible until an individual receives it by way of conscious union with God. The infinity of Truth, undiscovered inventions, sciences and arts of the future are available to any who are of the consciousness of God in search of such understanding to bring it forth. But these revelations only come through in proportion as an individual opens their consciousness to them.

Spiritual Truth is invisible before it takes form in consciousness then it produces an effect in the outer world. Therefore this Truth will free you of all mortal conditions of mind which means all conditioning of good and evil. Every bit of Truth you know will help to set you free from some phase of good or evil until through ascension you attain the fullness of that spiritual life in which *you* no longer live, Christ liveth your life. Unconditioned consciousness expresses itself as your being, body, business, home, relationships, finances, joy, peace, harmony.

137.

Prayer, meditation, communion, treatment and practicing the presence are those things that constitute praying without ceasing. It is living Life with the inner ear listening for God and the fruitage is the visible supply of your experience. If your fruitage seems to be getting less instead of more give yourself a once over because it is always something in your thinking mind that is stopping the flow of grace.

138.

God is the invisible, you are the visible but you are One.

139.

You cannot get away from your Self, you cannot get away from the God that formed you because it **is** your identity. God appearing as you and me **is** the secret of spiritual expression. God the Father made manifest on earth as God the son in expression.

140.

All is God appearing as form. The hidden secret identity of all is God and that is healing unto all who receive the awakening of Spirit to any degree for any length of time.

141.

Trying to preserve your life will result in your death. Every temptation reveals your weakness, your fears, that which you do not believe is being provided for you through grace-you are saying in essence you don't believe you are capable of complete trust, complete release of control.

Man thinks God too slow to do what *he* wants so he reaches his arm of flesh out to *get* it instead of letting the arm of grace **bring it to him**. What is gotten in the flesh can be lost, what is received by grace is eternal, can never be taken or lost but can be let out of consciousness, ie given away, shared without any perceived loss to you or your supply.

142.

"I trust you Father" is the most powerful prayer there will ever be. In those four words you give up all your humanhood, admit God is greater than you and that you will rest while it does what it does **for** you. This is the meaning of **Thy will be done Father.**

143.

What do you get from God that you can't get from man? Have you ever tasted true peace? Joy? Unconditioned love? That is what you receive from God and when you get these things of God you change because there is Life, joy, peace and love welling up within you and comes out through you and this is what you release as your nature or consciousness.

What does man give you? Duality. You may get gifts, occasion, things that you want and desire but the happiness, joy of these things are fleeting, always seem a let down when you get them but the feeling of God never diminishes, it can't, it is eternal where you are **in the degree of your surrender.**

144.

Don't forget the possibilities that lie within every moment. See the Life of God all around you; embrace it, feel it and let it flow forth.

145.

The human mind free of theories, fears, false conditioning, false concepts makes for a quiet mind in which the voice of God can be heard. When you can sit with no false concepts of anything in the world, no judgement as to anything, your consciousness brings all good to you. But it is only in proportion as you yourself **stop** believe "this is good" and "this is evil", "this is healthy or unhealthy" because that is no thing more that your mind presenting those forms for *your* acceptance or denial of reality.

146.

The power of God is the knowing of God and in this knowing of God you cannot bear to think of a time without it. That is the power of harmony, peace, joy, ease and supply because all you have to do is trust and rest, do and be, heal and reveal, release and receive. Rinse and repeat. What you are promised is what you receive if you put in the work given you to do. It cannot fail for it is Law but **you can fail yourself** by not adhering to the tenets, rules, principles of the Law knowingly sabotaging yourself, malpracticing yourself.

147.

God will always be there when you return from your side jaunt with duality because there is no sin too great for God to forgive. Why? Because God knows nothing of your sin, your human errors, so stop fidgeting at the door and just open the damn thing and walk back in. You erred and **the error will punish you** but God only knows joy because you are back where you belong.

148.

The power of God is in what God provides-everything. If you know **God is all you will ever need** that is the draw, the reason, the hook, line and bobber that keeps you with God and not man. God is reliable, dependable; God is Law. **The "power" of God is the Truth of God known in consciousness and the bond of oneness.**

The thought of being without God is like being asked to forget who you are and it is empty beyond measure, more empty than the life of man who has never known God because one who has known God then gone back to the ways of man is more broken because he feels acutely the loss of himself, his other half, his better half, his comforter, his solace, his best friend that keeps the cold away.

149.

A mind free of the belief of good and evil is the only thing that heals.

150.

In proportion as you persist in living good and evil, in that proportion are you mortal man. In that proportion are you mortal sense, forming your own world out of good and evil, want and don't want, love and hate, better or worse, me or you, stronger or weaker and as such, still grounded in duality, are nobody's healer. This is the literal Truth of the blind leading the blind if you believe you have power over the *devil*.

Why? Because unless you know God through awareness you are the blind leading the blind. **Until you truly understand why there is no evil in the world, why there is no power needed to fight evil, and why there is also no good to get you cannot heal** because you do not know God aright which is the Truth that heals.

Days 151-200

151.

When the mind receives the light of Truth the appearances conform more nearly to God's true nature. Consciousness is the activity and form of you so when the thinking mind is free of hypnotism, the belief in good and evil which is a fallacy, it receives illumination.

Remember the hypnotism of man is based on the (false) universal belief that there is God *and* that which is unlike the harmony of God and the mind of man, the human thinking mind, unknowingly expresses this universal belief which is the chaos, pain, lack, limitation and dis-ease of mankind.

152.

When your mind is free of the ignorance of man you see the world anew, you see God as all that is visible and invisible but if you are ignorant of Truth you will see only what is presenting as matter/material and not the Truth of what you are witnessing which is God substance in form; all of Life is spiritual **not** material in nature.

153.

When consciousness receives the light of Truth it conforms more nearly to God's pure form as an avenue of awareness of what God has created and is not the thinking mind that tries to physically or mentally correct error not knowing error is an illusion or false concept of what *really is* which is unconditioned God perfection in its image and likeness in form.

154.

Supply isn't divisible. God is consciousness/spirit expressing from the invisible to the visible that which is normal and natural to satisfy all need. Is there a need to feed 5000 people? Begin to break/share what you have and as much as you need will be provided with 12 baskets left over.

Your supply is not in the visible, that is the harvest or bounty. **Your** supply is in the invisible so do not judge by your senses what you have or do not have but know you are heir to the kingdom which is eternal and infinite as long as you are **of** the kingdom which is eternal and infinite.

155.

The thinking mind cannot create, it has no creative powers but when the mind is being used **in its correct orientation** it becomes an avenue of awareness for God to interpret the world for you through Truth.

156.

Sins are the result of ignorance of your true nature.

157.

I and the Father are one and while *i* can of my own self do nothing and while *i* of my own self am nothing, by virtue of my oneness **I** will meet every demand that is made upon me through Christ. **I** live yet not *i*, Christ liveth my life, the son of God, the **illumined** consciousness of all when known.

The knowing of this Truth is the key to the kingdom, the golden ticket, the back stage pass to where the real magic happens!

158.

Living in God isn't a chore, it is an opportunity for a lifetime of adventure!

159.

God is eternally imparting itself to you.

160.

Life seems real only because you cannot remember your previous Life with your creator, your Father, your comfort, peace, your solid ground. All God is asking is that it be with you once again, reconnected like long lost friends so glad to be in each other's company. This companionship fills your heart and you wonder how you had forgotten about this friend! How could such a loving friendship be wiped from your mind without even a trace?

You have amnesia induced by the false reality of man. Man does not know the Truth of their being therefore go on the only understanding they have-their senses. Humans sense their environment which create individual and specific physical and emotional responses for each person regardless of the good it is or is not for others. In this world of man each man believes himself more worthy thus consideration for others is sorely lacking.

Man thinks himself an island disconnected from all, trying to live as one in a world made of and by connections. Think Avatar movie in essence, the connection between all life being known, felt and honored and was the basis of their expressed nature/conscious understanding- they were firmly connected with their source and it was that way until in the movie man came to take what they wanted and could not understand the connection the natives had to their source. I'm not commenting on the movie, I am merely using a movie to give you a possible visual interpretation of a spiritual concept of connection by conscious oneness.

161.

Sometimes God is so silly. When you are with God you feel free, full, pregnant with opportunity, idea and are bursting forth with all of this as your expression in the world. God wants you to be bursting with all the flavor of Life available to you, supply in all forms, juicy and bursting forth with all the good things of Life. Be juicy! Let the grace of God, the love of God be the sweetness to another's life.

162.

All creation is finished and what expresses in your experience wasn't created *by* you rather it was created **for** you in the beginning waiting to be manifest, brought into awareness, for your purpose once you are back in oneness with God.

Man on the other hand thinks he creates his world but is only manipulating what already is within the confines of the human mind and this is Truth because the *mind* of man **cannot** create things in the outer world just by thinking it because none of what man "creates" is actually created/real rather is an illusion still of the *thinking* mind based on the *illusion human man can create.*

In the kingdom where there is only Truth, oneness, singularity of expression, all that is created is of God and God is harmonious thus is the only expression eternal in nature.

163.

Darkness and light are the same to God, in the eyes of God there is no difference between them, they are both concepts of man, temporal, temporary, of flesh because within the spiritual kingdom there is neither light or dark in any human sense, there is only spirit, that which has no similarity to what we know as light rather **light in the sense of illumined consciousness,** not illuminated *by* light like a flashlight beam but illuminated, uplifted, lit up, bright, shining with higher wisdom, emanating from within, bursting forth new Life.

164.

God's thoughts are not your thoughts because its thoughts are neither good nor evil, it knows only **is.** Who would say 2x2=4 is good? It isn't, it just is. It just is, like it or not like it, it is and will forever remain 4, is 4. You can hate it or like it but it doesn't change the Truth that 2x2 **is** 4. It is no different than any other is that is. You can hate it, like it, fear it, love it or loath it, but that doesn't change what **is.** Is is peaceful, easy, woosah whereas your *emotional/human reaction* to what **is** is what makes it good or bad to *you*.

It is this way man has changed the is of God to the personal perception of good or bad. The **is** of what **is** hasn't changed rather human perception of what is good or bad needs to be adjusted and that is accomplished only by knowning Truth.

165.

Faith is no thing, you can lose faith and not lose anything in fact it is better to lose all faith for all faith is blind, based on assumption or desire or someone else's Truth but until Truth is your guide and not faith nothing in your life will change.

Truth brings about a change in consciousness where you can let go of former beliefs because in the light of Truth you can see the error/unreality of the belief. Truth will never show itself to be anything other than Truth, is. Nothing can dislodge, change or usurp Truth for Truth is the only consciousness available.

If you have *faith* that God is real you have not had an experience of God to **know** God **is** real. Only an experience can remove faith and set in its place the rock of Truth on which to stand for eternity.

166.

Remember you are working toward living under the good, the grace of God and not under duality, the good and bad of man.

You are interested in living a life by grace which knows neither good health nor bad health, which knows only the continuity of harmonious being. A person with a healthy heart or disease free body never desires a healthy heart or a disease free body they are experiencing **harmony** without giving it a thought; they are, it is, I am. The ultimate of Life is when you take no thought for it, not for health or supply and let God live your Life. Just do it!

167.

There is no carnal mind, human mind, mortal mind. That which you have termed carnal or mortal mind isn't a mind at all, has no actual existence, it is merely a **belief in that which is not of God** and that has become your reality, the fabric, the operating system, the conditioning of your human mind as to what is good, bad, like, dislike, fear or desire.

168.

Being one with God puts you in a position of being a "witness." You do not actively participate but inwardly nothingize the error and await God's presence to heal the situation. It is in this way you heal without getting yourself enmeshed in error by way of mental or physical actions which are of duality.

169.

What you really are is all God is.

170.

It is not "I am good" it is "I am **is** good" (through you as you).

The qualities you express as your own are of the I am **of** you therefore always remember you of yourself can do nothing it is the Father expressing as you through you doing the work.

171.

There is no thing that can be called good *or* evil because there **is** only God. God alone **is** and **is as all** therefore there **is** no other.

172.

People talk about God as if God is in another universe you get to through death, some form of ascendence or by finding a way to this *other* universe. No matter where or how that is supposed to happen it is saying that *God is not of the same universe, consciousness as man.*

There is no other universe. This **is** God's universe just unrecognized as such because man is ignorant of Truth. Right here is the Garden of Eden **if so be** you dwell in the consciousness that **is** the peace and harmony of this state of consciousness called the Garden of Eden or heaven on earth.

173.

The worm of the earth becomes the light unto the world with no remnants of the past, wiped clean in the sight of God by your recognition and awareness of the God within and then living the middle path of **is**.

174.

In spiritual living you are never called to give of yourself **but to give of God.** You are not loving in and of yourself rather grace is flowing from you to those receptive to God. In the kingdom the only "things" you have are God's, never yours, for there is no you separate from oneness. In oneness which is wholeness how can there be lack? There cannot be so stop fearing and know because of the experience of demonstrated Truth that there is unlimited supply, abundance because **all that I am is yours** for the using but you yourself never *possess* it, it is given freely to you for your use but it should be given as freely from you as it was given to you.

In God's kingdom you have use of all that God is but so does everyone else in the kingdom/risen consciousness because all are **joint heirs of an indivisible Source.**

175.

Not doing so hot on your own? Get a personal tutor-God.

176.

The consciousness from which you act is the consciousness that is returned to you. Duality returns duality and harmony returns harmony.

177.

You are the Word made flesh.

You are the consciousness of God, spirit, in form expressing.

178.

Seemingly negative circumstances in life are not tests from God rather a bringing to your awareness the reality of your outward expression.

If you are reliving errors and worrying you are of human consciousness and the *sins* are punishing you by their *effects* because you are back living *duality*.

If you are experiencing harmony, love, peace and joy you are living in **oneness,** spiritual union with all that **is.**

179.

You of the higher consciousness are responsible for releasing this **internal splendor** so others may taste of the honey of God instead of the ash of man.

180.

God does not exist where human man is, God is only where it is known through conscious awareness and this knowing is the conscious union of you and God by way of the Christ of each man which is their very nature when they awaken to it within.

181.

Keep thy fingers to the lips (metaphorically) and let your Life bear witness/show forth the **practicality** of the principles of Truth when lived as your expression.

182.

God is felt as a presence that refreshes you from a never ending supply of Water from one Source. I have meat, wine, water and bread man knows not of, I have Life everlasting as long as **I know who I am.**

183.

The Love of God has no relationship to the way human man understands the word love therefore do not fear the Love of God because the Love of God merely means Self completeness and it feels like you are floating, joyous, peaceful and completely satisfied in all ways. This is the feeling of **God's** Love, **God's** allness expressing and has nothing to do with you personally except that you cannot help but express the way you feel within which becomes your Love of God expressing to the world so they may know what it feels like to be Loved in the true sense of the Word.

184.

If you aren't comfortable using the name **God** because of your history call it what you want as long as how you address **it** is of the highest reverence, deferment. You can call it a human name but understand names you know are of man and of duality and that is why for some the name God cannot even be uttered or thought because of the conditioning they have experienced thus associate it with.

You do what you need to do to make yourself comfortable in this transition as long as you are not changing the Truth about God and you are walking the spiritual path. The name matters not, the intent matters all. Just be and all will come through revelation for your peace.

185.

The only power is invisible and it is of one expression-Self-which is harmonious, good, peaceful and abundant.

186.

Always remember regardless of human condition or conduct of any individual, the seed of God, divinity itself, is within all. The fact that they haven't awakened to it does not change this Truth. When you have awakened to God you honor your bond by seeing the true self of all and grace is your return for doing the Father's work.

187.

Can you see how the life of man is filled from birth to death trying to be and do and become where the life of spiritual man is resting in the knowing of who they are which frees them from the responsibility of taking thought for their lives to experience Life under grace.

188.

God dwells in man as a habitual state of being thereby creating oneness which is praying without ceasing.

189.

To have communion with God get comfy and ask for something akin to this:

I know nothing Father, but I want to. I want to know you, I want to be with you and have harmony peace, joy and supply! I want you, your smarts, your patience, your kindness. I want to understand what illusions have been blinding me to Truth and I want to understand why Truth is so darn hard to find!

190.

As you lose your fear error disappears.

191.

If you want God to work in your life you have to relinquish control, defer willingly grateful for the lifeline and let God take over the navigating while your thinking mind rests. You let God **give** you the direction you are looking for, the know how to do it and the connections/oversight to make it happen. When you are with God you are not in charge, you don't need to be so just take a breath and let God go first in all ways.

192.

Father break through the self of me that I can be made free in Thee.

193.

There is no power outside of you, all power resides within and must flow out but it cannot until you release the hold, the power the world has on you. **You have to be ready to leave the world,** be tired of all it gives and be willing to "die" to it every minute to live in the harmony of God consciousness knowing Truth.

194.

The only thing you can change is your perception of reality and the only way to do that is by changing your understanding of God by an actual awareness of the presence within.

195.

"Dispel the illusion Father, show me Truth." Then get quiet and listen for God on the field, in your awareness.

196.

I is supply within you unfolding outwardly as you need it, think Niagara Falls as your outgoing manna and the 4 great lakes as the source, God. You don't see the source, it is invisible to you but what you receive in your experience is of the invisible source.

197.

Anything other than harmonious flow means there is something in your mind you need to address ie reveal error and receive Truth or just a simple "your way/will Father not mine," or "your grace is my sufficiency," take a breath, maybe stretch and then get back to it. In every situation where you are trying to do that *which God is not a part of* you will feel frustration, confusion, anger, fear, anxiety, panic etc, which merely means you have allowed error to be entertained momentarily as a reality. Heal it and get yourself back in the kingdom. Easy peasy, all is as it should be once again.

198.

You are that spiritual man if so be you desire wholeheartedly the spirit of God dwell in you because that is the siren call that opens the door and allows God to enter in and fulfill itself in you as you.

199.

To see without taking thought is to see through the eyes back of you, the Father's eyes, through the consciousness of Truth which dispels illusion because if the Father is present in awareness that is what you experience.

200.

Every time you remember the Father within you are giving a specific treatment which corrects the belief (remember you always treat yourself, not your patient) that you are alone, separated from God.

Every time you remember the story of the branch connected to the vine/Tree you are giving a treatment for immortality, wisdom, support and supply.

Days 201-250

201.

You may get asked this question by man and it can trip you up as a new ascendant. The question in one form or another is *"where is your God and why does he allow all of these horrible things to happen if he is so powerful like you say?"*

One reason only: **God is only where God is known** and if you don't know God you live in the chaos of the world, man's world of chance, good and bad with no understanding of how to change it.

There is a God but until it is operating in your experience **by being known to you,** until you have a conscious experience and subsequent awareness of the presence of God it can do no thing for you or the world.

It is only when God is the Life of you are you able to understand the errors of man to understand why there is such horror in the world. It is with this knowing you are now of that allows you to be an instrument for good to change the expression of this world from chaos to peace.

202.

There are many expressions of mortal/human man but only one expression of spiritual man.

The question is and always will be "how do you go from man whose breath is in his nostrils, man of many expressions to the singular expression of good, God in awareness?

The answer: keep knowing Truth and that is the atmosphere of One.

Knowing Truth ie keeping the mind stayed on God, being in the present moment **is** continuous prayer, the singular activity of spiritual man. Spiritual life is simple, easy and fruitful because there is no opposition and no opposites therefore there can be no friction/chaos/disharmony because all is of God. Life with God is harmonious, without chaos **because God is too pure to behold inequity** which is anything other than Self which is perfect harmony.

203.

Stop fearing the unknown, the unseen, the invisible. Remember that which is real is **invisible,** that which is *visible* is unreal, illusion, mirage, falsely identified as *matter,* being of a *material* world therefore anything sensed by your physical body is not real, unreliable, fickle, changeable, undependable, chance.

204.

Anything said or thought concerning *i,* i need, i must, i can't brings you duality but if you say **I** and mean the Father and not you the human personality, if you say "the Father is the I of me and I don't live by bread alone" you have brought yourself under grace because your only desire, the only thing the little i of you desires is to be with the big I, God.

205.

Every time a discord comes into your experience just leave it alone, don't address it, don't react to it because it is no thing more than smoke, it will clear from your view if you know rightly what is being presented to you. You realize what is being presented is under the law of cause and effect but because you are under the Law of God, grace, **it has no power** to "make" you do anything, react to it because the only power there is **is within you** and this knowing is what frees you from the chaos of man to live peace, harmony and Love with God.

206.

Cosmic law is the entirety of man's existence. God's Law is the entirety of spiritual man's existence.

207.

You are under either the Law of God/grace or the law of man/cause and effect; you are always within one consciousness/governance or the other but not both at the same time. By your consciousness is your Life manifest.

208.

Don't pretend to the world how sanctimonious you are when the only one you have to convince is the Father within and there is only one way to convince the Father within and that is not with words or thoughts but by a mode of life that conforms to the Sermon on the Mount.

209.

A spiritual healer nullifies error with Law and does it through grace.

210.

Human man has *accepted* the beliefs of the carnal mind but human man is **not** carnal mind rather the *carnal mind is the atmosphere of man believing he is separate and apart from God.*

Carnal mind isn't a *thing* it is a **belief** relied upon *as* Truth in the absence of Truth in human consciousness. *Carnal mind operates on and through the belief in more than one expression* therefore if you know the Truth of One you express as One thus are living in the consciousness of God expressing Truth which is harmony not chaos/duality.

211.

God constitutes all being therefore the nature of all being is God substance in form.

212

Don't try to use God, don't try to use Truth, don't try to *overcome* sin, disease, lack, limitation and death you won't succeed anymore than the religions of the world have succeeded. You cannot do it. This is why psychiatrists that are trying to find out what the error is *in* their patients can't succeed-**the error is not within man, it is the atmosphere of man,** the belief in both good and bad powers acting upon them because of who they are, where they are from, because of their economic status or for any reason man can think to blame their current existence on.

The only thing that will help man is to know that which is not known to them and that is the Truth of their nature. If one is of a mind that doesn't feel like it belongs on this earth, have been seeing therapists for years because they felt there was more to life and that this life felt fake, they would be told they needed a lot of work *to learn how to live in the "real world"* or "this is the only life there is so you have no choice but to fit in and make it work." You feel crazier for trying to fit in than you did being yourself though odd to the world.

You are not crazy for there is no crazy in the kingdom only in the world of man. Does having a mystical experience immediately change your life for the better? Absolutely! Are you going to see results out in the world right away? Possibly but I will tell you without any reservation you will begin to feel validated in knowing there was something you knew existed but couldn't find and to the world it was viewed as a medical neurosis, a mental disorder, a failing of the cognitive ability, bad coping skills but it is the soul of you seeking Truth. Unbeknownst to your thinking mind when you came into this expression you were already on the hunt for Truth and this time of expression is a continuation of that conscious seeking to get you over the hump, out of man's unreality materia medica wants you to believe is an illness to be cured when it is a longing to be satiated.

213.

Remember the curious get milk, the thirsty and hungry get meat but before that as you are learning it is secret, sacred and silent, only grace in your midst attests to the changes going on within you until you are strongly grounded in Truth to withstand the mockery and perceived impracticality of living the spiritual life.

Why does man think this living is impractical? Because how could you live in a world where you do not pick up the sword, all are your brothers and the reality of being is harmony not chaos? That is crazy talk! Man cannot understand this and that is ok, you live by your Truth and man lives by his beliefs and though they do not mingle you will be instrumental in bringing illumination to many in darkness just by living the **impractical** life of God.

214.

Most people think when they are forgiven all is forgiven. All is forgiven by God but not by man. Sorry Charlie, karma follows you like cat hair until it is dealt with. As you do what is necessary for your sin whether it is forgiveness or jail time, start this moment in the consciousness of God to do what is given you to do to clean your karmic slate and soon you will begin to outwardly reap what you are sowing to the spirit. Don't wait until you are done dealing with your karma, **God helps you through the karma** because that is your consciousness **now** if you are practicing and studying. By you being **of** the consciousness of God you become a light to those you are around and you may be asked what you know that makes you chill and not angry or vengeful.

215.

They will try to tell you this is blasphemy, that it is the devil trying to lure unsuspecting souls into its trap. Who is **they**? Man who doesn't know God. That right there reveals all you need to know. They. Human man not of God knowing so why would you get rocked in any way by man ignorant of Truth that you **live** every day?

How many people have told me this was total bullshit but had read no further than the tenth page before making that judgement? A lot. Not because they truly believe this isn't Truth but because their humanhood rejects, pushes away, blocks their ability to accept Truth because they are not of the consciousness to accept Truth, have not experienced enough of the pain of human living to cry out for something else. Know it for what it is and heal the situation by bringing grace to bear, let Truth begin to awaken thy sleeper to begin their own journey which will then allow them to accept Truth without rejection ie ego coming in to argue what *it* believes in the face of what **is**.

You cannot discuss/juxtapose Truth to belief because Truth **is,** is **is** the only reality therefore it **is** and can be no other. You can explain Truth to one who is open to accept the Truth you are revealing but nothing you say through the lips will ever change a person's beliefs into Truth therefore you do not engage, argue or try to prove your Truth in any way to those who hurl stones.

You are never asked to defend God through the lips you are only tasked with expressing God in all situations and only when man is done living on bread alone will he search for the bread of everlasting Life and find you who is the expression of that which they seek. It is only at this point can God be talked about because it isn't discussion to *validate* God but **learning** Truth by which to live.

The only way others will find their way home is through your expression of God in their midst by which to become aware of that which is not of man's expression-peace-that begins their search for what is missing-God.

216.

Never tell someone to be more loving or generous or forgiving because they cannot be anything more than they are now until you know Truth for them by realizing that those qualities *are not of the form, man* but of **the Source of good.**

What is the source of all good? **God known in awareness** which is the wholeness and allness you experience which becomes your expression which to man is you having/being these qualities because you are expressing them.

Only when you are **aware** of God are you able to express God which is love, kindness, benediction and forgiveness which **looks to the world as if *you* have become more loving, kind and forgiving.** *You* are not these qualities, they are being expressed **through** you as you because you are of the source of these qualities ie God consciousness.

217.

Fulfillment comes only when you are living, moving and having your being in God.

218.

Parents are the instrument by which God brings you forth into expression. They are caretakers, those given the responsibility of your mind, body and soul until you are out of the wilderness and strong enough to stand on your own feet. But you must awaken to the realization that it was God that sent you forth to earth, God that sent you into being for God's purpose, for a spiritual purpose and this study of God is to find out what that purpose is.

Scripture tells us clearly we were sent here to show forth God's glory just as the heavens declare the glory of God and the earth shows forth his handiwork. You, we are the greatest creation of God therefore glorify God by being alive not in your humanhood but in your Christhood.

219.

You are never further from God's grace than you are from your own I. That is why you don't have to earn God's grace, you don't have to deserve it and you don't have to wait for it.

God's grace has been with you always **and with the awareness of it** are maintained and sustained, eternal, immortal, clothed, fed and protected.

To know God aright is life eternal. No man knows God aright until they know God as I. When you know God as I you know the one word that is neither objective to you nor subjective, is not external nor internal to you but **is you, constitutes you and sustains you.** To know God aright is to know that the I in the midst of you am mighty, I in the midst of you am God.

220.

What you experience in the world as good or evil is a **suggestion** taken as reality and suffer the effects, the karma returned upon you because of your belief in two powers.

People who have been told they look ill by more than one coworker or acquaintance in a day soon are sweating, coughing, having chills, checking for a fever etc. What this reveals is the ease by which people are subject to the **their own biases, fears and judgements** which is nothing more than self hypnosis brought on by world wide mesmerism held as Truth.

221.

Life becomes a completely different story when you do not have two powers, when you find that you don't even need a God to get rid of the evils of this world. Where the spirit of the Lord is there is freedom (from the duality of man), where the spirit of the Lord is there is liberty-physical, mental, moral, financial. Where the spirit of the Lord is, where the consciousness of God's presence is, where the feeling of this presence **is** there is liberty from every form of discord.

222.

The evils of this world come to you via invisible suggestion and you can prevent it. You can prevent it by starting your day's activity with the realization **this is the day the Lord has made,** this is God's day and I am God's being and this body is the temple of God and my business, my household, my family is the temple of God and I live and move and have my being in this temple of God awareness, consciousness.

223.

All that is necessary for harmony is God's grace realized. You don't have to know a lot of deep metaphysics, you have to know the simple things such as one power instead of two, know by way of experience that God is more than a three letter word, more than any synonym man could think to come up with and all would be wrong because God is an *experience.*

224.

Never think for a moment attaining your physical health or physical wealth is going to make you one bit happier than you are now. If anything it is very apt to increase your unhappiness. The answer to this Life is coming back into the garden of Eden where there is neither health nor disease, wealth nor poverty only a continuity of joy, harmony and peace, a state of **is,** a state of **being** that is God in awareness expressing as and through you.

225.

There are no enemies for in reality the enmity you feel is coming *from you because of how you are interpreting the situation from personal history/biases with personal survival always the goal.* The Master knew right well that the enemy wasn't the other person or situation but the belief in two powers. The enemy is formed in the *mind* then expressed outwardly and this is what greets another in the human world, the complexities of survival invisible yet felt, acted on or responded to thus perpetuating a cycle that isn't even real but of thought that becomes action and reaction until you have the Hatfields and McCoys on every street, every state and every nation.

226.

When you say "thy grace is my sufficiency in all ways" you have to mean it, understand what you are saying and why you are saying it because it is revealed Truth. You mustn't say thy grace is sufficient *to give you money or health or anything separate and apart from God.* No. Grace **is** the sufficiency, the allness of God in action as your Life and you will find when you have God you have so much more than the world could ever provide.

227.

God is universal in nature but must be known individually in that God is everywhere God is **known.**

Only individual man can chose God and in doing so becomes the instrument through which God may become universally known.

The individual spirit is the instrument by which God will be known universally.

228.

You are under the laws of man while you are taking advantage of an eye for an eye and a tooth for a tooth. As long as you are *resisting* evil, as long as you are *using* the weapons of the world you are under the law and the very knife you throw at someone will come right back to pierce you in the chest-karma, cause and effect.

You are under the laws of man when you indulge in duality and there is no way of expecting grace at the same time. You can pray for God, grace for a million years and it isn't going to come to you because you can only have grace when you **give up the weapons of the world.**

229.

The more grace you personally facilitate to mankind the more grace is returned to you and this almost continual release and receiving of grace is what creates the harmony unto your life. In the beginning of your journey grace was here and there, you knew you were on the right path. The more you studied, practiced the presence and healed error the more grace you could definitely identify as coming into your experience because your life was noticeably smoother, easier to breath.

Now your constant contact with God is a natural state of being meaning you and God are open to each other pretty much all the time thus you are releasing grace pretty much all the time which means grace is constantly coming into your experience to the point there is no stop and start rather harmony is your expression because God is more consistently your nature.

230.

Talking about God out in public is like showing pictures of your colonoscopy to your boss-not the right audience.

Secrecy is a spiritual principle and only the adherence to spiritual principles keeps you in the Garden of Eden and brings grace to bear.

231.

What becomes of God and devil, good and evil, immortal and mortal when you no longer have the belief in two powers? They disappear and you are left with God which was the only reality from the beginning. Why hadn't you seen this Truth before now? Because you were not ready and because you were not ready it was *veiled,* not of your consciousness to understand because you were of man's consciousness of duality and not of God consciousness of oneness.

This is the difference between human man and a mystic: a mystic doesn't try to understand the words rather lets God imparts the meaning of the words **back to them** as revelation, Truth in awareness, the aha moment or bazinga! I get it now! Thank you Father! Hugs!

232.

The religions of old spoke of God *and* Satan, in the metaphysical it is immortal and mortal, in philosophy it is good and evil **but there are no such powers** except to man of earth who thinks himself separated from his good, his support, his direction and purpose and is trying to figure it all out on his own.

233.

Harmony is what is felt when grace is as constant as possible by way of just being your nature, being one with God. God is your favorite blanket, a bowl of yum, your favorite movie and your bestie kind of vibe up in there and it is more than you have ever known from a human relationship. Yes, that is what this is so treat it as such-a sacred, secret, silent relationship of the deepest commitment that **is** your happy place.

234.

If you do not take up the weapons of defense on your own behalf you cannot be injured by those weapons. If you do not meet out justice according to human standards then human justice cannot come back at you. What you bind is what enslaves you and what you loose is what frees you.

235.

God alone is your good, your supply, you fortress, your high tower, your rock and your resting place.

236.

The spiritually enlightened never know death, never experience death. Their passing from this stage to the next isn't an end but an awakening into a higher state of being/consciousness.

It is only a mortal, man of earth who experiences *death* but it is only temporary because he comes back into awareness as the same consciousness of mortal man he was when he died.

The whole purpose of being in this form is to begin the quest to find God and rise in consciousness to live as the prodigal son returned home living Truth.

You are given every chance to break the cycle of returning as a human by choosing God this day so that when your time of transition arrives you will not come back as *human* man rather **spiritual** man **knowing** your Truth to **live** Truth.

237.

You have been searching lifetimes to get to this moment. You have arrived home without having to leave your house. You have arrived at

Life everlasting, eternal freedom. You have found the secret of Life. Your knowing God aright **is** the Holy Grail, the Fountain of Youth, the meat, the wine, the water and the bread of Life unto you.

The mystical experience is also known as the coming of Christ, the same as how Jesus **came to be** the Christ. When you are conscious of God within you have an awareness of it and are one to the degree you desire to be in oneness with God.

238.

The ball was in your court getting to this point and it will always be your serve. You are in control of this relationship. You keep it alive by being of it or not. It is that simple and that cut and dry. There is no leeway, no wiggle room and no excuses because God is impersonal Law. Nothing changes Law therefore God cannot be other than it is. It cannot leave you for it is your nature but you can forget your true nature and stop hearing God by choice.

239.

Everything you see, hear, touch, taste or smell exists as an effect because it is the result of something you are aware of as being **outside of you.** Now that you are understanding there is neither good or evil in an effect you lose your fear of it, you cannot fear something that has no effect anymore than you fear a sunrise. You not only don't fear a sunrise you can't even love it. You can enjoy it and benefit from it but no one yet has fallen in love with a sunset nor hated it or feared it. It is. You just take it as it is for what it is.

The Master felt the same way about leprosy, he didn't hate it, he didn't love it, he went up and touched it and showed he had risen above the *belief* in good and evil. He knew leprosy wasn't good but he also knew it wasn't bad, it had no power but the power the thinking *mind* of man gave to that which they were ignorant of-all is of God and there is no dis-ease when Truth is known.

Man names things to explain them but in doing so gives them added qualities that end up completely changing what is to what is not. By adding to what **is** you are changing **is** to conform to your *personal perspective* thereby giving it power that it does not have in and of itself.

You give power to *things* through erroneous belief but there is no thing in this world that has any power to do anything *to* you, not even what man calls death. There is no power in the world unless it comes from the Father within and this Truth is what makes it possible for you to free yourself from this world of cause and effect and place yourself squarely in the arms of grace, good.

240.

When you aren't receiving God's harmony it isn't God's fault it is yours for blocking it. How do you block God? Think duality, act duality, think me, mine, little i. This is when you feel *human* again, full of emotions and fears which keep you from receiving God, the things of God. It is a vicious cycle that can be stopped at any time but it is only you who can make that choice.

241.

You overcome the mesmerism of the world when you stop using the weapons of man.

You overcome the world in proportion as you overcome the belief in and use of good and evil in your life because you are experiencing Life from a higher state of consciousness where now you know there is no good and there is no evil, there is only God being, is-ing which is harmony in expression.

242.

Thinking doesn't make anything real only living out from what is real brings reality into expression.

243.

There is no time in the consciousness of God.

When did 2x2 *become* 4? It has always been so. When did apple trees *begin* to be apple trees? From everlasting to everlasting. All is, has always been and will always be. There is no beginning and no end for the Life of all that is **is** eternal harmonious expression of Self be-ing.

244.

You have to be at a point of conscious awareness that allows you to accept Truth that the presence you feel within **is** what man calls God. It is at this point of conscious awareness when you feel/sense/know there is something within you, not **of** you but separate, can have conversations **with** and **receive** from this source the things that make your life easier, smoother and more what you envision life to be.

This that is within **is** the holy grail, the secret of Life, the Water of Life eternal. It was never a *thing* to be found outside in the world but a Truth to be **revealed** from within.

245.

This experience comes to each in your own time and it won't come no matter how much you try until you are ready for the experience. Remember God is lining this whole shebang up for flawless execution with you at center stage but you have a role to play and that is **listening and being receptive.** The experience will come and it is this readiness, willingness to be before you have proof that is the reason why you will go to the next step of oneness with signs following.

Signs following means grace, the allness of God in your experience and is a measure of your devotion that comes the more you study and practice spiritual living. It is in this way the Truth of God's existence is made manifest in your experience as the good things, the added things and the needed things which are called the fruit, harvest or bounty of Life which is God in expression.

246.

This may seem like a hard road but only because it is a complete 180 in 1) who you are 2) how you "do" life. It becomes a life lived in quiet contemplation with God, an inner life that is secret, hidden from the world of man. It is your silent friendship, the new love you keep hidden and know this relationship is the allness unto your Life. You cannot think of being without this inner friend of peace, insight, Truth and companionship because you realize without it you have been living as a husk, a shell, non existent but for visible form.

247.

There will always be appearances that you will need to treat. Remember treatment is always for **you,** not the patient, student or client. It is for you to bring Truth to the error presenting **to you** to bring grace to bear. The more you dissolve false appearances the more consistently your consciousness is open, is stayed on Thee because every treatment reestablishes God in your consciousness as the only Truth which reveals the Truth of error as illusion, echo.

Soon you will begin to feel it within, sense its presence in your experiences because you are now aware that there is a pattern, a path, an overseer setting things up for your ease, joy, effect of good. God and I have made this into a game I call breadcrumbs where I am able to look back and see the confluence of events of seemingly random happenings that led up to X and know I had nothing to do with its coming into my experience ie the orchestration, the harmony of its expression was all God.

Once you can follow happy accidents backwards you are ready to start playing the breadcrumb game. Something innocuous happens, catches your attention, it may have felt odd, stands out in some way. Then something else, then nothing for a week and you drop your little conspiracy theory musing with an "I'm going crazy" complete with finger twirl and low whistle. Next day something happens and the instant it registers you know it is the breadcrumbs falling into place and viola! God made the crooked places straight and grace paved the way. Thank you Father!

248.

You don't need to believe a bit in God, the name, and especially don't believe what you think you know. To benefit from God, to have good in your experience all you need is a desire *to know God*.

249.

My own shall come to me.

You may have been born into ignorance (duality) but you are ignorant no more. Truth has been revealed, God is Truth in your midst when you have an awareness of God within.

250.

Jesus the Christ came to reveal the Father's kingdom is **not of this world.** This has led men from the beginning of time to think that because God's kingdom **is not of this world,** it is not of this universe, this time therefore is **not** available to *man* where he is.

Man doesn't understand God is not a physical thing to be in *proximity to* but that which you are to be **conscious of** right where you are.

Days 251-300

251.

When you experience peace, joy, love, abundance, laughter etc, you are feeling God; that is what God feels like in expression and it is this expression of God which goes out from you as you bringing others into the atmosphere that is God because it is inviting, warm, safe, gentle- everything the world lacks.

252.

You cannot use God or Truth. You subject yourself to God making yourself a servant, not a Master. You don't make yourself a Master over evil with God at your back rather you become a servant unto God and the evil disappears. Why?

Evil is that which is not **of** the nature of God, it is **unlike** God but you know there is no thing real that is unlike God therefore evil doesn't exist where God is known because God is all there is.

It is all there in the New Testament but it must be understood **not** through the conditioning of orthodox religion rather **revealed** to you by reading the New Testament with an **unconditioned** consciousness that is open, willing and eager to learn from the soft, small voice within.

253.

You have to experience the Bible as God reveals it through your own consciousness, the omnipresence, omnipotence and omniscience of

God back of you interpreting the words so they present in their true nature of meaning and not merely the words written by one of higher consciousness that makes no sense to man without God awareness. What you get when you go within to be with God is conscious understanding **at your level of understanding.** God doesn't just dump Truth on you, serve it up and wait for you to make heads or tails of it.

God gives you what you can understand in that moment. What you receive and another receive are going to be similar on some points but vastly different in scope and depth of understanding depending on the degree of oneness with God. **You receive at your level of understanding and that is why this is a progression of higher and more illumined, God filled states of conscious unfoldment.**

254.

The human mind is shifting sand, duality. Consciousness is The Rock on which I stand. You must step from the sand onto the rock, out of duality into oneness to find sure footing in God, universal creative consciousness.

255.

Silence=receptivity=grace in your midst.

256.

To be spiritual man is to wear no costume rather what is seen is God as you-open, kind, loving, benevolent etc. There is no inner man and outer man to spiritual man, there is only one man and that is spiritual man ie what you see is what you get because there is no other way to be therefore there is nothing of me that isn't front and center to you- I am, you are and if there is discord it is because you are ignorant of Truth-that there is nothing to fight for, struggle for or desire when you find God **because God is all that you desire** just not in the form at the moment of what you desire. You have to learn to desire the Source, the **cause** and not the *effect*.

Yes you might want outer stuff but to want outer stuff as a spirit means to rest in the fact that it is God's good pleasure to give you the kingdom and that in your conscious oneness with God you are of the kingdom. If *you* desire and act you may *get* on your own humanly but it will be a fickle pickle, sour one minute, sweet the next because it is based in duality and not God.

God is never fickle, God is steady as she goes, stay with God and you will be fine on this journey because with God you are **of** God. Without God well, you know how that goes.

257.

Ask to know God, desire to just rest in all that it **is,** the eternal comforter. Ask questions, let its Word work to bring forth Truth in you. You are cultivating a relationship, you are having an experience. An experience by definition changes you, changes the way you perceive the world, yourself and every God experience you have is to give you the vision of the eyes "back of you."

258.

Have you forgiven yourself and others 70x7? Are you going to God free of human baggage? If not go and forgive then come back with clean hands.

Do you pray for those one would call an enemy? Those who despitefully use you? If you do you are of the Christ mind, living in heaven and expressing your love of God as your love of mankind **knowing all error is illusion, ignorance of Truth and in that knowing release grace which is the healing unto mankind.**

259.

You can feel yourself yielding to God when you realize your negative emotions and knee jerk reactions are lessening. You feel through awareness to be in an atmosphere of peace, evenness of being, harmony and in this state of being can silently say "go and sin no more." That is the forgiveness of God speaking to you but only because you have died daily to the beliefs of man and **know** the Truth of God, Life eternal.

260.

What is the most clear and concise way to explain to one who is interested in living Truth how to understand the difference between human man living duality or spiritual man in oneness expressing God?

The only difference between man of earth and man of God is this:

Man of earth believes there is good *and* there is evil, that one triumphs over another resulting in the conditions/consequences they experience. To man there are *powers* against him that he must push back twice as hard to keep his ground and maybe gain a little beyond that. God to man is something not really believed in but when all else fails, human thinking, send up a prayer for what you need done.

Spiritual man knows there is but **one** expression of good/harmony that **is** God, Father or Creator. Spiritual man knows God exists because he has had an **experience** of God within his own being. This experience reveals the nature of your true self as that of Spirit, an individual expression of God in form known as spiritual man. Spiritual man lives by/through the consciousness of God guided by three simple principles. This abiding in God, deferring all will to God instead of using your will brings you more and more into the knowing of God and to the degree you know God and do the will of God is the degree of grace in your experience.

God is no thing you can think with your mind, God is impersonal, spirit, Law. God is Law. God is harmony. The law of God is harmony. Law is that which is always, perpetual, infinitely the same, cannot change, is. Gravity is. You may think you can alter gravity but your mangled body will tell the Truth-you cannot change the expression/effect of a Law no matter how hard you try. Therefore the things of God are eternal in their good because God is good and God is Law.

God cannot take because God doesn't give. God isn't a person, doesn't think like a human. God is impersonal Law given a human designation of a higher being than man for man to ascribe to/reach for/emulate/become and in that vein there is an equal sign in the equation of God. The degree of your conscious oneness with God equals the degree of grace in your experience.

Want more? Spend more time in the consciousness of God by knowing only God **is,** all are your brothers, forgiving 70x7, die daily to the errors of man and be the expression of God to the world ie harmonious, peaceful and benevolent. **The degree to which you love your fellow** man and desire above all else for them to know God is the key to the kingdom of heaven and all the riches therein.

261.

The state of consciousness of the healer is that of a free flowing expression of God in all ways. There is only good, is, God; all else is an illusion.

262.

You are either in or out. Being out is hard, being in, once you understand the Truth of God, is the easiest thing you could ever do because to the degree you give up **your** will and desires for the will and desire of God is the degree of God's grace/supply/allness unto your existence. Win/win.

263.

God doesn't *give* you a happy sunny day; God **is** your happy sunny day. All that **is** your Life is within you, your expression flowing out and back to you as that which God wants to experience. God realized is fulfillment, is the harmony unto your being, the success of your day, the cement of your relationships, the stability and reliability on which to stand in every and all situations for God is as all situations when God is living your experience.

264.

A true seeker knows what they seek is greater than man and therefore cannot exist where man is so the search **isn't so much a what but a where.** Where is there love, peace and harmony? Where can I rest and where can I commune with that which is higher than man, higher than all that is known? Where do I find this creator of all? King of kings? The most high? Where does it exists?

It is in the invisible. But how will you know it? It will be felt. It has a presence you will know to be real as you experience the experience, feel it as a sensation within your being, expressing to you in your language of understanding the answer to each person's search for Truth- that there is a presence within every man that is the Ancient of Ancients with no beginning and no end encompassing all that is. This presence when recognized as Truth unto your being returns you to your nature of spirit in form, God expressing as you through you.

Now that you know where God is you know where all supply is in whatever form is necessary for your continued expression of the glory (love, abundance etc) of God shown forth as wealth, abundance, harmony, peace. It is within you and is brought forth into expression by your conscious oneness with God and as a result of this oneness the sharing of grace with the world.

So how do you access all that is of God? What is the magic word? The key? The key to the kingdom is asking to know God, have more love, more peace, more wisdom, more understanding, more patience and how to love those who seem unlovable so all may be brothers instead of enemies.

To get God all you need do is rest. You give every person in your consciousness to God and never let a whisper of worry cross your mind **because God has them because you have God.** You rest in God for everything from grocery shopping to navigating human relationships, you trust God to go before you to make the meeting or event good for everyone involved because what you want as an outcome in all situations is God-harmony, peace, joy-and you want that for all mankind therefore when God is on the scene you are not the only one receiving God's grace, everyone around you has the opportunity of benefiting by **your** God consciousness and receive some form of God that fits the bill specific to each person.

How do you stay in God consciousness? How do you keep your mind stayed on God all the time? Honestly it is very simple. To have your mind stayed on God merely means not thinking as a human-not worrying, gossiping, judging, desiring, comparing rather you are empty of those things of man's world and are **present,** not thinking of the past or the future but here, now, seeing the beauty in the trees, hearing the laughter of humanity and if there is error you know what it is and what to do about it-nothingize it.

To be in the consciousness of God is to be at peace, be living the expression of Self completeness experiencing harmony and abundance. God is eternal and you are of God, of God consciousness therefore there is nothing in the kingdom/your consciousness that defiles the kingdom/is a lie/false/illusion therefore when you rest in the consciousness of God, good, that is the cause **and** effect of what you experience.

265.

There will be times you encounter something of the world that is confusing to you because of what you have been accomplishing in your life with God; you thought you were getting beyond the human bull pucky. You are, you are suffering much less than you used to so take heart! as you rise in consciousness you succumb less and less to the things of man because as you rise in God consciousness you lower your incident of discomfort/error in all ways.

Even Jesus the Christ suffered pain and he was **risen, illumined,** he was high enough in consciousness he wasn't coming back to this form of expression again, he was going home. And yet he encountered pain, fear and maybe even doubted for a moment so yes, you will experience things of man but the degree to which they negatively effect you decreases as the degree of your conscious oneness with God increases.

Understand Jesus the Christ willingly accepted his human death **because it was for the purpose of showing the world the reality of resurrection and everlasting life when God is known in awareness through the transcendental mind or Christ consciousness inherent in all.**

The life, death and resurrection of Jesus **the** Christ was for the **purpose** of revealing everlasting Life with God for mankind **to witness, desire to understand and learn** what it was that rose a man from the grave. Jesus is a visible expression of the **metaphorical** death/rising you experience which is a **change in consciousness** that transitions you into your everlasting body.

It is **not** a physical death and rebirth as given of Jesus, it is meant for man to grasp the meaning of "you must die to have Life eternal." The dying is in consciousness to the duality of man to rise as the singularity of God in expression.

Jesus was the first to be witnessed as the Christ byway of his resurrection **but all will be risen and renewed through the knowing of the indwelling Christ because Jesus the Christ was meant to be the way shower of the prodigal son returning home/union.**

266.

God created all in the beginning and all is available in consciousness. No thing is ever created by man rather everything is revealed through consciousness which then comes into expression through you, the instrument of God in the visible world once again proving all is God in substance and form.

267.

On the spiritual path *you* do not create your good rather you open yourself to the indwelling Christ, the same Christ of Jesus, to reveal God's infinity in your consciousness which is the source of all good in your experience.

268.

Ask daily for more of God-more love, more joy, more peace, more understanding, more patience and definitely more Truth!

269.

The goal of spiritual living is to get to the point where you are no longer held down by the desires and wants of the world but desire that which is above, beyond, not of the world of man to rise to. This is done by the realization in consciousness that God is not out there separate and apart from you but within.

You get to the point where you are willing to leave all that man gives-chaos with a sprinkle of good just to keep you hoping-to receiving all that God has for you. What God has for you is within you and can only

...to manifestation when you know the Truth of your-
...th of God are one in the same.

270.

Spiritual life isn't a cold way of life but can look that way from the outside because of the non reactivity to the world around you while others see fires burning in every direction.

271.

The entire teaching of God lies in the secret teaching of the word **I. I** am all ... the meat, wine, water and bread unto your Life (when you are) under grace.

272.

You don't get rid of evil, you free yourself of the illusion, universal mesmerism, duality by knowing Truth. To get rid of something implies it has reality/Law behind it and all error regardless of the appearance is an unreality, an illusion because all error is based in the mind and not on what is actually out in the world.

273.

What is the nature of all sin? Duality, human man expressing.

What is the nature of harmony? oneness, God expressing.

274.

Error is universal and experienced in different degrees by individual man depending on their level of conscious understanding of the laws of man or the grace of God. Only man can free himself but in doing so prepares the way for more to be freed thus at the appointed time all men will free themselves and it will become at that point a **universal freeing of individual man back into the one consciousness of God.**

275.

Spiritual power is knowing **is**-the consistent, constant, perpetuation of Self, which is harmony/good/God in expression for all eternity.

276.

Christ is the revelator revealing omnipresence within each man.

277.

No one can use power, it is invisible, of God, the only true expression however when you willingly submit to God's **governance** you are under the Law of like begets like in your experience and the more you defer to it, do as bidden the more you live the expression of the Law you are under.

God is the only is-invisible, singular, creative and is the substance of all that is visible, that which **is** its unqualified state. You experience the glory of God as harmony, peace, supply, love-but you are not receiving *material* form, there is no such thing because everything is God substance, invisible spirit manifest. There is no matter in the universe only

God expressed in specific form which man has named as elements on a periodic table which to man are the building blocks of this *material* universe.

But where did the elements come from? The one creative expression that **is** the universe. Elements are merely the different forms of God named by man by which to classify and categorize what they experience, find or discover.

278.

Man fights what isn't real because man doesn't know what he fights for/against is only a concept of his own perspective based on the desire to have, be and survive. There is only one power operating in consciousness but man does not know of his **consciousness,** he only knows of the thinking mind, the *conscious* mind, the reasoning mind that man thinks is that which defines each man from another-who *they* think *they* are.

Understand there is a difference between your *conscious* or thinking mind and **consciousness** of being. One is of man and the other is of God.

True consciousness is an enigma to man for man rarely goes beyond the thinking mind and that is the issue to solve. You cannot hear impartation to receive revelation unless the thinking mind is quiet of the world.

279.

Human is a label for that which is not real, has no Substance or Law behind it to make it real because it is a *concept* based on a false belief of man being separate and apart from God.

As human man you do not exist, you appear to exist but you do not begin to **live** until you know why you exist and then you can live that existence of Truth because when a new name is taken you become that name in expression and that new name is Child of God, joint heir to the kingdom.

280.

Have you ever wondered why all of life, when man is not present, is harmonious and self sustaining? Because the mind of man with his duality and illusions of life have not entered the virgin ie man free environment thus this virgin environment exactly reflects God's harmony of life and it is perfect.

When man interjects himself into any situation, man being one of duality/judgement/wants and personal need, all results/effects are skewed by personality, too many cooks in the kitchen and soon everyone is fighting for what they want regardless of another.

Let Go and Let God means to stop all thought, just observe silently and let the natural order of life take place because it is the introducing of personal desires that mess this whole world up. Why? Because this world was created for God's expressions to express Self, harmonious living dependent on God and not the world, your job, your families or your intelligence for your survival.

What has been left out of your education about Life is that this isn't your reality. You were never supposed to depend on any one or anything of the world, let alone yourself, eek! The pressure! You are to be dependent only on your source, God, universal creative consciousness, what the world calls God.

281.

God governance is gentle and kind, not of or by force, coercion, punishment or banishment. God is divine Love which is the fulfillment of Life.

282.

Good doesn't come *to* you, good is **revealed** within you when duality/chaos is removed.

283.

The easiest way to start letting God, good, love, grace and harmony begin to flow through you is this:

For one week you keep track, just a tick on a piece of paper or mentally, of every time you judge, criticize, condemn, get frustrated, lose your temper, think thoughts other than kind, for any and all reasons. If you do it, own it. This is not to prove you can be unkind, we all can be, but to show you, prove to you God can change your life and all this talk isn't just talk, it is Truth, the deepest Truth you will ever feel. The purpose of this is to show you when you get on the path how these expressions of duality lessen ie you go from putting three ticks on your paper a day to three a week.

I can honestly tell you what Truth feels like-home, welcoming, warm, relaxing, safety and security. It is the world solid beneath your feet, a rock to stand on knowing that rock is there infinitely. It is the whisper of the purest breeze that wraps you in a cloak of grace and you feel the presence of the Father, "I got you Child, I got you."

Oh, crying now. Did you feel something in your body when you read that? Are your lacrimal glands working overtime? That my friends was your soul, the Christ of you so completely grateful for being seen you felt it stir. Did that feel delicious? OMG!

Sing it with me, "this is how we do this ... !"

This feeling and more can be yours for the small price of surrender. Surrender to God your desire to be, do or have the things of the world and ask for the things of God-love, harmony, joy, peace, companionship, patience, benevolence.

So how do you get that feeling again? You live in the consciousness of God where peace is. To live in this consciousness you have to die daily to the consciousness of the world, know Truth of error and nothingize it. **Your conscious union with God brings that feeling back** into awareness because that is what God feels like in your midst. Yes God has been with you since the beginning but until you **know** God aright through an actual **experience** of God within that part of you is not accessible to your awareness thus there is no God in your experience just duality.

284.

Reasons don't matter in this life because reasons are excuses. Spiritual man does not excuse his behavior, he asks forgiveness and takes the karma incurred knowing it is just a little duality stuck to the bottom of his shoe, wipes it off and gets back on the middle path of is.

285.

I is your salvation and supply but you will never see it. Living in the realization of I you will see its effect-signs following-ie better health, relationships, supply, life experience.

286.

On the wheel: going around and going nowhere.

Human life is fruitless, it is the constant motion of standing still/going no where, living and doing all day every day only to wake the next in the same general place. Even a big event that sways your pendulum of good and bad will even out until you are once again standing still in constant motion; the going around and around each day going no where.

The orientals call this being on the wheel, man goes around and around and around but is standing still/not changing consciousness to change the standing still to progressing/movement, actual living of this Life as it was meant to be lived.

287.

God appreciation is gratitude which supersedes the appreciation of man meaning the feeling of appreciation from one of spiritual knowing will be felt more fully within as Truth when received whereas appreciation from man can feel not so appreciative but it is because they have no God in awareness by which to share gratitude.

288.

There is only one infinite spiritual being appearing individually as you and me.

289.

God reveals errors in your life so you can receive your good. Sometimes the moving and shaking can be painful physically and/or mentally even financially but if you have experienced the grace of God as good in your midst you know you can trust the process because you trust God to be the good you are to experience.

Keep trusting, keep healing and keep asking for understanding from within and soon what was is no more and the world is completely remade in his image and likeness-harmony.

290.

Because you listen for God when God comes in through impartation you have to be ready to be active ie listening implies learning which for me is writing his words down as they come to me. A lot of time mid conversation out in the world something triggers God to start talking. I put up my finger and excuse myself. I have had people say I was rude, dismissive so I try to let those close to me know if I put up my finger and walk away it is because God is talking and I have to pay attention.

God just said in that instance when I put up my finger to say, "excuse me I have to take this call" and then leave. How funny is that! Such a good way to excuse myself because everyone does it so it isn't rude but of societal norms.

This is just one more little joke between me and the big Guy which makes our relationship that much deeper, real and experiential. You will have yours too and they are just more joy in the treasure box of God called living under grace.

291.

Wisdom comes to you from within, a revelation from God sudden and without taking thought. Joel calls it the thunder of silence; I call it the whisper that shatters the darkness; the name matters not as long as you know when God speaks Truth is revealed and it is to bring you to a higher conscious understanding of Life.

292.

Walking a path that isn't yours is painful. Being human is not your path that is why living as human man is painful.

293.

Mrs. Eddy: Mortal mind isn't really a thing, it is a term denoting nothingness.

Mortal mind is no thing but a concept denoting a belief in being separate and apart from God which is the atmosphere of man who believes God is out there somewhere to be prayed *to*.

294.

An illusion in thought, a mental image, has no substance, no reality, merely an unfounded belief, superstition or rumor. If you give credence to illusion instead of realizing the nothingness of illusion you have made the illusion a thing in and of itself to be gotten rid of where it was nothing to begin with! Oh the extra work that must be taken to undo the nothingness you turned into a personal reality just to dispel it again as if it were a *thing* instead of right from the beginning knowing the **nothingness** of what you were envisioning and move on, no thing to see here.

295.

Prayer is not human words or thoughts but a silence in which you **receive** God's Word. Prayer is also a way of life in that you live **by** prayer ie a listening attitude.

296.

Life is God, spirit, immaculately conceived ie Self created therefore everything comes from this Self creation not as *matter* but **Self** in form visible to the human senses.

There is no such thing as matter, there is only God in awareness which is the substance and form of all that is visible and invisible.

297.

Man cannot envision a different world because he cannot envision a different self but spiritual man is drawn to find that which is the Truth of their being thus their journey is predicated on becoming different than they are.

298.

Few men believe, fewer still practice and fewest are those who have had the mystical experience which is what you are learning to achieve.

299.

There will come a day when evil no longer finds expression because it will be crowded right out of the atmosphere as more and more people attain spiritual understanding of their true nature and begin to know God as the only presence, that all are your brothers whether they are expressing that nature right now or not.

The earth will be so full of the knowing of God in individual awareness that they won't have any choice but to come into this spiritual atmosphere because the atmosphere of duality will be erased from the minds of man.

300.

Consciousness forms and governs itself as that which is visible and invisible.

Days 301-365

301.

The power of God is the promise of is. Is is constant, Self perpetuating eternal harmony.

302.

With or without God? It is always your choice. It is work for the first year, you are relearning how to be you, process the world around you from a different perspective of oneness and not duality. It takes study and practice to get your light a-glowing to become the light unto the world which you are when the awareness of God has dawned within.

That is what starts the flow of grace in your life, the click in awareness, the dawning of understanding, the revelation and realization of God within.

303.

To say God is a *jealous* God is verbiage from the Old Testament but it merely means though shall have no other God ie you give no power to anything outside of you. It isn't jealousy just cut and dry **with me/ without me.** It is always your choice but if you chose God, one expression, that must be your expression and not a suggestion. God will not be mocked ie it is God's way **or** man's way.

304.

Paul called communion with God "praying without ceasing" and to the degree you do this you succeed in overcoming the world-the illusions of the world-and rise above duality to Truth which is your power of oneness as your armor, your protection, your impermeability to man's shenanigans.

305.

All you need as "protection" for the day is just to remember Truth: all is God, there is nothing but God and in this knowing you walk the path of perfect peace.

306.

You can never ignore outright or shake discord and inharmony, you can never be rid of them until you realize they are **constructs** of the human mind, it is the functioning algorithm of man who thinks himself flesh and destined to die.

307.

There is nothing preventing you from being a transparency for the infinite nature of God, God imparts impartially to all who are transparent, receptive to it.

308.

God: my consciousness will be your consciousness but my consciousness does not nor will ever compete with the consciousness of man therefore until the thinking mind is quieted, the receiving mind, consciousness, cannot discern what is being received thus receives no thing from the within, no Truth, no thing of God, good.

309.

How do you break the hypnotism of man? By knowing that hypnotism isn't power rather a suggestion of one mind over another; it is merely the suggestion, belief that one mind can have control over or be controlled by another. This suggestion of power, this hypnotism of mind is merely the carnal mind fearing for its existence-if my mind can be taken over I must protect myself first. This is fear and it is the basic tenet of human existence.

Man uses the sword to try to carve out a slice of life completely unaware that instead of a mere slice he could be gorging on the all of Life.

310.

Man's belief in a life separate and apart from the awareness of God has forced man to account for his own life. Man has created his own sense of finite nature but it is no fault of yours, of individual man, it is the universal mesmerism, conditioning, atmosphere of human man save a few who know Truth.

311.

It is only the fear of perceived power that gives something power. If you know all is God and say "I see your glory in every creation and there is no thing to fear for **I am of you** and all of Life is **of** me therefore no harm can come to me no matter what the conditions of my existence look like to the world, I will fear no evil for God is the only reality."

312.

To pray for your enemy doesn't mean you are asking God to prosper them in their wrong doing but **to release sin and discord from their consciousness for it to be felt by them as an experience of God that brings Truth in the form of relief, release** so they may put down the sword and pick up the shield, put on the robe of **is**. You aren't just releasing your enemies, you are releasing the enemies of nations, those who have offended nations, races or religions when you bring God to bear among man where God was not known.

313.

In spiritual living there is no such thing as competition. There is no such thing as someone taking from you that which is yours *except in the human picture.*

Certainly there are times we are instruments of wrong thinking by which error manifests. That doesn't make you evil, that just makes you ignorant of how to protect yourself from mesmeric influence by way of living the spiritual path through right knowing of:

Truth

Awareness

Treatment

Practice

314.

It isn't the words that do the healing it is the consciousness of Truth **of** the words, the knowing by the one of higher consciousness what the words do **for you** not what the words *sound* like to human ears that *interpret* through good and bad, face value.

315.

There will be the temptation to use some human means to overcome lack.

By using human means to solve a problem you lose your demonstration of God therefore what you receive for your efforts will be only what you worked for and it will be of duality. If you had just rested back and remembered that with God you have all you need because of the infinite supply of God, you would have received that which is perfect for what you are to experience.

The temptation of abundance lies in what you think about the abundance. You realize God is good and it is coming to you from every direction but you begin to focus on what you *have* and not the *source* of it. You begin to hoard your abundance or pick and chose who to help and how you treat others. You are once again back in duality without even realizing it because you are focused on the *effect* and not the **source.** In this way the source is not available to you because the source exists only in your consciousness. Therefore you are back to fighting and scraping because all you had of God, good, is gone and you are once again trying to manage chaos.

What happened? You stopped knowing the Truth of supply. **Supply is the added things unto your relationship with God.** If you stop having a relationship with God you lose your avenue of supply. By behaving as if the money was *yours* and not **God's** you began to treat it as *your* money. This isn't to say you don't buy for yourself, treat yourself and your family and friends, of course you do as the spirit moves you to do.

As the spirit moves you to do. That which is received by grace doesn't belong to you, you are the recipient of it at the moment and have it eternally if you chose but it is God's. **You lose your demonstration of your oneness when you begin to take credit for what is now pouring into your life.** Your didn't *do* anything to receive it, your love of God released it into your experience to have, use and share because there is a constant supply of good as long as you are conscious of the source of all that is good-God, not you of your own might, power or thinking.

A lot of people who enter the path find a rebirth of the body and sit back and rest in that health, coast in it, stop paying attention to what brought about the rebirth/metamorphosis. They feel *they* did something to attain health rather than the "health" of the body being a result of their relationship with God. They forgot the source of the metamorphosis and begin to take the changes for granted; they feel healthy, they are healthy and will continue on this way.

They do not understand that they attained a healthy body **only because they were tabernacling/resting in the silence with the essence of their health.** They do not understand the spiritual relationship, oneness **is** the health of their countenance because in oneness the nature of your form is God. Therefore if the spiritual relationship is **not main-**

tained the health that is here today may only be the health of youth and it may only take a touch of age to turn that health upside down.

Temptation comes to you in many forms but if you do not recognize it as temptation, little temptation by little temptation drops you from heaven. Why? Because you are denying the very source of your freedom from error/duality by *doing* instead of trusting God. Get to know the signs of temptation.

Temptation comes from outside of you because of something you still think *you* need because you don't currently have it or you desire that which God has not brought to your knowing. Temptation is of man who does not know the storehouse of Truth within himself thus does for himself what God would release freely, without work, without thought, without the hand of man.

Temptation is not a trick of the devil, temptation is not God's way of tripping you up so you can suffer. Temptation is you coveting that which you do not have at the moment. **To covet is to reveal the consciousness of lack.** Lack is not of God so you must be expressing from man. When you are faced with temptation, get that thought in your mind to do something STOP. Just stop. What are *you* doing? *You* are doing and that is the problem. You are thinking of a way to get something by your own hand, might and power.

But if God is your supply why do you need to do anything to *get* your supply? Ahh, that's right. You don't if you know Truth. Just smile, feel God smile at you within for having figured it out pre error and say "thank you Father for always reminding me of my Truth so I may rest and receive."

You discard as if worthless your spiritual consciousness, throw it away for the temporary enjoyment of something of the world of effect. You bar yourself from the **allness** of God when you desire that which is not of God to give.

316.

To spiritual man there is no such thing as a miracle, only God in your midst in form and function for your unfoldment and is a matter of omnipresence-spirit where spirit is known. All is God when God is known in awareness.

317.

The sooner you take the first step on your path of spiritual living the sooner you will see signs following as peace, harmony and joy in your life, in and of the people around you and then as the needed things of living as supply in whatever form is needed for your continued unfoldment as the expression of harmony you are.

318.

It isn't what is in a book that benefits anyone, **it is what the reader does with the information** in the book-study, practice, meditate, treat, repeat. You pick up your bed and walk by the effort you put in. You are freed of your erroneous beliefs by the steps you put upon the spiritual path.

A teacher or healer can help but progress only comes with you doing your part of the relationship which is walking the talk, living Truth as your expression which is harmony to the world. By your expression are your returns; it can be no other way.

319.

All healings are merely the revealing of Truth by bringing God into the awareness of one receptive to Truth-God is and God is within you not outside of you.

There is only one Truth of being and it makes itself known to you in the degree of your willingness for God to govern your experience from now until the end of days.

320.

When you tell God you are done with this life you may mean you are ready to die, be gone from this world but what God hears is **you are finally asking for God, for renewal, for right knowing of self as Self.**

The only reason I know Truth and am able to share Truth is because one day I told God I was ok with leaving this life. Yes I loved my children, my husband and family, had work and hobbies to keep me busy **but** in and of myself I was lost and confused and so damn tired of trying to understand life. Why am I here? What is my purpose? I could feel myself being drawn toward apathy, the death knoll to joy.

It just boggled me that no one could tell me **why** I was here and living with no understanding of **why** was torture to one who needs to understand, to find Truth, to be that which is authentic, real and true not made up. That is the reason I didn't really care if I was or if I wasn't because what did it matter if I was if I didn't know **who** I was or **why** I was?

God being God doesn't know death so what God received when I said I was ready to leave this life was **I want to understand You, Truth. I am done with this life, please take me from this life (of human living).**

I didn't know it at the time but even though my prayer was to a God outside of me I was asking for what God could give- Truth of Self and by my admission that **I knew nothing** I was giving consent for that which was **not of this world** to become active in my consciousness to the point where I can now teach the meaning of Life to those like myself who search in earnest for Truth of being in which your purpose is revealed to be experienced.

When you say you are ready to *die* to this world for whatever reason understand you will not receive what you are humanly asking for but what you need- **Truth** in awareness which is the answer to all you seek.

321.

All awareness is conscious awareness because only that which you are conscious of are you aware of. If you are not aware of what is going on in your ex fiancé's brother's cousin's life, you have no consciousness of your ex fiancé's brother's cousin's life ie you don't have any thoughts about your ex fiancé's brother's cousin's life. It doesn't exist in your consciousness, it is not a current, conscious thought waiting for recognition as "being" of you.

322.

Don't be so busy being good that you miss being great. This is the problem with man who has found out how to have most of the life they want and it is good, you are good, kids and work are good and you like this place you have carved out for yourself. But you are missing out on being great, not of yourself but your Life, your livingness. You are complacently happy when you could be rising to the stars in wonder just by knowing and learning to live with God at the wheel.

323.

I has never been man, I has always been I. I the Father and I the son, not i of individual personality because there is no such thing as your consciousness and my consciousness for consciousness is God when rightly known.

324.

Christ awareness is transformative to the human condition.

325.

The *human thinking mind* is the processing center of man, the decision maker, the interpreter, judge and jury of life because the mind seems to have abilities to discern what is good or bad for it and wants to decide for others as well. It has become a "reasoning" mind, a mind with the ability to weigh things out, reason the consequences and then make a choice as to how to proceed for maximum self benefit/survival.

This is the error of man. The mind was not meant to think as if the controller of you but as an avenue of awareness for God, I, not i. It is a deductive mind that receives through impartation the work to be done for the Father by the Father as you doing the works, being the know-how, being you as you perform that which is given you to do.

You don't *think* of what you are going to do beyond what is normal and natural for you to do ie work, home, family. **That which is to prosper you will come from within to your conscious knowing** and God will lay out your spiritual journey from itinerary to lodging, enjoyment to quiet contemplation. You are just along for the ride experiencing the good stuff of life when you let God be the teacher and you the student.

All of this life when it is lived righteously is that of teacher and student, Father and child. You do as your teacher instructs using its conscious understanding of what is to be done and the way is imparted to you. You don't have to know anything beyond **who** you are because all that you will need to know will be given through impartation.

326.

There is only good and bad in the world of man but grace abounds where awareness rests in God.

327.

The power of the human thinking mind is destructive because it is of individual expression which is duality and duality is no thing real which makes the power of the human thinking mind no power in effect/experience.

The power of God is constructive because it is of singular expression which is always harmony in effect/experience.

328.

God awareness breaks all material and mental ties as claims of power or reality.

329.

What is faith? Faith is living the Truth of God in expression before you have the experience of God as Truth.

Faith is **knowing** that what you are learning and doing **is** Truth and that Truth will come into expression as **known** Truth through an awareness of the presence of Truth within your own being.

When you have had the mystical experience your faith is no longer in the words of man but cemented by conscious knowing thereby taking faith to knowing which is then lived in expression as your Truth.

330.

By practicing the presence of God, keeping your mind stayed on God, on the things of God and not of the world you will begin to get the deeper meaning of Truth because you are reading it with a spiritual eye ie God is interpreting the meaningless *human* words as the Truths they actually are.

Only one of God consciousness, a mystic, can understand what is written by another of God consciousness because to man the things of God are folly, don't make sense ie the complete error of man trying to live by the words in the Bible instead of the consciousness back of them that brought them into being. The Bible wasn't meant to be taken at face value it was meant to be taken in for God to tell you what it means. God reveals the Truth of the words humanly read so you are not dependent on *words* but on **Truth.**

331.

I talk a lot about answers received from within. What are you to do with them? Pay attention to what is received, not just that it was received. If it is to forgive your debtors release them consciously and move on. The answer is both the answer and the action, the study point by which to Live the Truth until it become Truth unto you. I am finding that not only do we peel layers like an onion but God wraps his answers in layers of conscious understanding.

In the beginning of this new way of being the answer received is taken as given ie go and sin no more, there is no lack in the kingdom, all I have is thine. Then as you progress, understand more of God consciousness you realize the answer is also an action, something to remember **to do** ie get up and walk, sin no more, release debtors as you go forward to remind yourself what you are not to do if you want to stay within the consciousness of God under grace.

332.

you cannot save the world, it has been ruining itself from the beginning of time and will continue to until this world has been overcome but it will only be overcome by those who live in God, who live God as a reality thereby dissolving the universal mesmerism of duality.

333.

There is more power in the silently spoken word than the spoken word. Begin to rely on the silence more and more for your guidance, direction and peace will be with you.

334.

Your good is an unfolding experience within your consciousness and not dependent on anyone or anything but on your **relationship with God** for that is the measure of your return of grace.

335.

Stanford Dole: Dole pineapple

"Prayer, in its highest exercise, is an opening of the gates of the soul/conscious awareness to the divine influence, to the mind of God."

336.

The only error is in your mind.

337.

It is you who carries peace into the world, you are the instrument by which God's grace reveals peace and harmony. Without you it is lost just as it almost was in the days of Jesus. Were it not for those who knew the Truth of God, of the indwelling Christ, the Word of God in awareness, the Truth of being would have been lost. Without the disciples of old, without the disciples of now God would be lost to man's knowing.

God's grace is enough to save this world when you understand what grace is and how to benefit your experience and the experience of the world by it.

338.

You don't need the feel of God on the field when you live with God in awareness/on the field therefore when you heal it may not always be a sensation of a presence but a realization of Truth that just comes into awareness as a Truth revealed.

That which comes into awareness is God's conscious knowing which is your conscious knowing therefore it feels as if you thought it but it is God expressing Truth through you who **knows** Truth.

When you have been in oneness with God for a while, have a real relationship of teacher to student or Father to child, when you are more with God than away/out of the consciousness of God the more automatic is your conscious knowing of Truth so you receive of it effortlessly.

In this way realize how far you have come to be able to let God flow without your thinking mind wanting to be part of the action. It is the metaphorical **stepping to the side, letting God go first** that is the reason you experience God more and more as your expression. You have come to the place where the effort of your study is rewarded in that you have become what you were studying and practicing.

This feeling of being where you are supposed to be, being who you are supposed to be and living out from that expression brings God into your awareness and that is why you benefit by spiritual living.

339.

God cannot step out of its orbit and come down to man, man must rise in conscious awareness to the knowing there is a plain of existence, degree of consciousness where the Truth of your existence is revealed as child of God.

340.

Christ consciousness is harmony embodied where you are.

341.

The world doesn't know the nature of God is harmony it only knows the nature of man-survival of the fittest.

342.

Spiritual living is a journey and you will make mistakes, see illusion and get pulled into it rather than treat it, commit transgressions against yourself and others and forget momentarily who you are and revert to the duality of man and pick up the sword. It is ok! I have to say sorry to Father at least once a day because that judging thing just doesn't want to leave me completely!

No one walks before crawling because all of life is learning and releasing that which you do not wish to embody anymore as your expression. You are allowing God to express as you to experience the fullness of the visible world without being involved in the chaos of the world.

343.

Thomas Hobbes-hell is Truth seen too late.

Now that you know what Truth is hell becomes a choice.

344.

God is warmth. Just step outside of God for a while, go back to duality for a bit, be rude, see error and respond to it then feel the feeling within. It is unsettling, empty and cold, like the sun has gone behind a cloud. Just treat yourself and you will be back in the full glory of God's warmth.

345.

The reason for spiritual living is to know God not for the prize of health, wealth, job, supply or abundance.

The realization and awareness of God as all brings all of the added things necessary to your expression-not man's interpretation of health, wealth, enjoyment or adventure but the allness of is, is being God, perpetual eternal good/harmony unto your experience.

346.

What you experience of human life-sickness or lack-is but an opportunity to prove God **is,** to make a demonstration of God as your being in which no sickness could ever be found, an opportunity to open your consciousness to some vital Truth that will change the entire course/direction of your life, a chance to live peace instead of chaos.

347.

Inner spiritual harmony appears as outward health, wealth, harmony and supply. How you express to the world is a direct reflection of your state of consciousness-God expressed is grace in your midst, duality expressed is duality returned.

The more Truth lives within you the more you become Truth which appears to the world as health, wealth, joy, harmony and peace.

348.

You will still at times speak of "problems" in your life but you don't see them as *problems* rather when you think "problem" it should be immediately followed by the **opportunity** to treat, bring grace to bear where no grace was. Problem dissolved. Not removed, not ignored but returned to its rightful place of nothingness.

349.

You live by every word that comes out of your mouth and when you are in oneness your mouth is the revelator of the Father within. Your words reveal Truth and the earth melteth-the awareness of God releases error back into its nothingness.

350.

You must leave your nets-your dependence on the world for supply.

You must leave your mother and your father-universal mesmerism you have imbibed as reality.

You must put all your trust in God because that is the only Truth in which to put any trust.

351.

Now that you find yourself in this reality of God love you have to learn how to assimilate/live in this new environment. That is accomplished by reading, studying, practicing and living what you are learning and soon you will be swimming along completely immersed in this new atmosphere that demonstrates its allness to you. Soon it will become your nature, normal and natural, and you will understand through experience the *old man of earth* was the unnatural state of being and the **new man of spiritual knowing** is your natural state of being.

352.

You are here to enjoy, commune, grow and experience God. The things you now experience in God consciousness are given freely for your enjoyment but are not to be coveted, hoarded or desired like man would/does for fresh manna falls daily ie God is and God is eternal so if God is today then God will be tomorrow.

The allness of God is as constant as your oneness with God.

353.

What keeps you from demonstrating God's allness? The attempt to get something, to desire something outside of the desire for God, to want something or believe you have earned or are deserving of something.

You cannot demonstrate supply. You can only demonstrate God activity in your consciousness which appears as supply because it is of God and not you personally. Supply comes byway of you only in so far as you release the activity of God within to flow out and then back as bread on the water, as supply without the hand of man. God's supply may come by way of another giving/sharing/selling something to you but the reason for it is God, your oneness with God.

Remember conscious union with God constitutes your oneness with every being and thought therefore any person, of God consciousness or not, will be used to bring grace to you in visible form. It doesn't come *by* the hand of man but *by way of* man to you into your experience from the only source there is.

Do not take credit for supply, God will not be mocked. All supply is God; there is absolutely no supply outside of you that hasn't come from your consciousness union with God and you can gauge your depth of relationship by the amount of duality you continue to suffer from or the amount of grace you are supported by.

354.

I know God is the health of my countenance, the Life of me, the allness of me because I know I am I am.

355.

Spiritual healing isn't a negotiation, you are not asking, begging or pleading your case to God rather you release your claim of perceived error to God for God to tell you what truly **is**. This is the only way to know Truth-when it is **returned** to you from within. That is the only Truth.

356.

Protecting self isn't crossing self/making the sign of the cross as a warding, it is knowing Truth.

Purify yourself-die daily to the illusions of man

You aren't *becoming* spirit, you **are** spirit returning to your true nature after living erroneously as human man separated from God in conscious knowing.

357.

Spiritual messages and visions are revelations, Truths revealed by God that come through/to an individual from within.

358.

Orthodox religion separates man from God whereas true Christianity, Christ consciousness, is union with God.

359.

You don't go into communion for a purpose, you go into communion for the **experience** of God. The experience itself **is** the healing agent to all error because it is the peace that passeth understanding and brings relief to the weary.

360.

The human mind cannot reveal spiritual Truth because the mind isn't real as it is being employed by man. The mind of man is not a creative mind but a deductive mind to be used to perform that which it is given to do from God within, impartation. Only the consciousness of God as your consciousness allows your mind to become the deductive instrument of God it has always been ie in conjunction with, not separate from or in opposition to God. You need your mind, just not in the human capacity of thinking.

361.

Man with no awareness of oneness, no feeling of home within themselves will always search out in the world for that which will make the insides happy but it can't be found outside of you. This is the erroneous circular nature of unnatural life that confuses man and enslaves him to the unreality of duality as his experience of life.

362.

The relationship you have with God is the relationship **you** create.

363.

In the awareness of being spirit, God individualized, what you receive from God is yours for as long as you want it, it cannot be "here today and gone tomorrow" if it was by grace that it came to you. In this way there is no chance, no "gone tomorrow" unless you release it by choice for the benefit of another. You can never not have supply if you know the source and nature of supply.

364.

It costs you nothing to be kind, generous, loving because all of those things are God's to give through you but they are not *of* you, not yours to give or withhold but flows out from you as your expression so if you are angry and bitter and don't believe in God you have zero God flowing through and out from you thus the constant return of duality.

365.

What you embody in consciousness, God or mammon, is what is expressed to the world as you/your reality of being/who you consciously know yourself to be.

Extras because that is how God rolls!

366.

The pain of loss isn't the pain of what is lost it is the pain of **you** being lost. You are lost because you believe your happiness can be found out in the world and that is the illusion of mankind.

367.

The garden of Eden is a poetic expression of/for the nature of God-good, perfect-and is nothing more nor less than a **state of consciousness**. This state of consciousness is the conscious awareness of the Christ within, the seed of God within each form called man. When this state of awareness through actual experience of the God within has been achieved you release all you ever believed to be true about yourself and others and learn a new way of expressing-as individual expression of the one true God instead of human ego/personality.

368.

Labels and judgements:

Humans don't understand anything that doesn't have a label, a designation, a judgment attached to the root of **is** so man is unable to process/conceive of a world around them without labels.

Labels are merely place holders and man finds their place among the labels they ascribe to others by contrast or similarity. Labels create a hierarchy of importance, worth, recognition as you compare yourself to other labels which reveal your own sense of worth-I am thin, you are fat, you are smart I am dumb, you are successful I am poor.

Ooh, another word of man's thinking mind-competition. Why do we feel everything is a competition, comparison? Because society dictates you must compete for you place in this world. Who told society this was true or was it manipulation of the masses for the purpose of control through competition, proving the strong over the weak as favored? To keep you always striving, looking, wanting and desiring the things of the world to improve your personal labels?

Competition for man is for personal gain. Who told man he must be other than he is? Who told him he wasn't pure of spirit, devoid of inequity? Who told man he wasn't good enough inside so he must prove it on the outside? The impersonal universal mesmerism *that to be you must get.*

Man is wired to get accolades, acceptance, notoriety which means when you try to prove your superiority in any way that which is employed to get the job done will come back to smack you in the pocket book, marriage bed, job status or dis-ease in some form. What goes around comes around is the Law of **like begets like** thus you cannot escape your good deeds and you cannot escape your bad deeds because all deeds are under the Law of karma.

369.

There is no genuine emotion, no selfless act among men, ever, it is impossible because of the duality which is their operating system of living.

370.

The nature of my peace is God. Peace descends; it is not found or gotten. It is an awareness which is your assurance, your Truth that reveals **I am with you always.**

371.

It is the belief that spiritual man can express in any other way than harmonious/good that throws spiritual man into the second chapter of Genesis which is all about the life of spiritual man *separated* from God in conscious knowing.

This separation in conscious knowing is termed human or mortal man and with it the appropriation of **I** as *i* expressing as individual ego or personality **separate and apart from Truth.** In this world of spiritual separation you don't find the God of Love as the creator but something called *Lord God* and Lord is synonymous with law not Law. In other words in the Old Testament you are under the *law of man,* reward and punishment not the **Law of God,** grace in your midst revealed in the New Testament.

When you are living the first chapter of Genesis you're of the consciousness of creation, of God, under grace, love, allness of being, having only the consciousness of God, good, harmonious living within so every act, every response, every cause and effect are of the same nature, good, for there is only good in harmonious living otherwise it would not be harmonious right? In this atmosphere of God consciousness your life is supernaturally guided. In the atmosphere of man you are guided only by desire, primitive instinct and personal history by which to formulate a "plan" to live by. Man is a post it note with a line from baby to old man with a big question mark between the two.

372.

Man wings it. That is all they can do, wing it, spit into the wind and hope for the best.

God consciousness takes all that chance, worry and fear off the table, wipes the spittle from your chin and leads you one step at a time, gradually so as not to send you running for the hills, to his loving arms where you can let go of error, know Truth and live Truth-oneness with God.

373.

Your sins can only be removed from you when you stop doing that which brings the sin upon you. Neither do I judge you but go and sin no more lest a worse fate befall you. Your choices create your life, that of peace or chaos, God or man, eternal life or 3 score and ten.

374.

As spirit you are of a whole, like part of a hive, a closed system of support, maintenance and supply unto itself infinitely and eternally.

375.

You are not *protected* by God in the way man thinks of the word. Your protection being with God is the not being in the world experiencing duality. If you aren't doing it you aren't subject to it. It is that simple. If duality is no longer a part of your consciousness that means you have outgrown those experiences of life, that consciousness of being and know no dirt, no sin, no lack, disease or fear can be *of* you for there is only one thing you are of and that **is** spirit.

376.

When you chose to rise above the human laws of cause and effect you are no longer under the karma of human man rather within the allness of eternal existence.

377.

The nature of error

The nature of human man is duality, expressing more than harmony. Human man cannot change his nature. He may try to deny parts of it, ignore, push down, try not to let it bother him etc, but at some point human nature will be revealed because man cannot *change* into other than what he is, only God in the awareness of human man can do that through revelation/revealing of Truth.

Only God can reveal man's true nature as that of spirit. Understand this isn't you trying to change your expression to be a better *human* it is a revealing of **Truth** that has always been.

How do you go from human to spirit? You need a bond of Truth, a covenant on which to stand and express from and that is God within waiting for the time you want to know it.

378.

Think of your thinking mind as a glass full of dirty water, the dirt being duality causing turbidity, turbulence, cloudiness, uncertainty. As you begin to understand spiritual living, die daily to the errors/illusions/

maya you are now realizing to be erroneous thinking, the water in the glass begins to clear, is less murky, less turbulent, less uncertainty.

The more you study, imbibe Truth, release error and have more constant awareness of God the clearer and clearer the water gets ie you are emptying out the duality of man that clouded your mind and letting the pure water of everlasting Life be what you are filled to overflowing with which becomes your expression to the world which is the expression of knowing God aright which is harmony of expression and experience.

379.

The saying goes "God is a jealous God" but I would like to rephrase that in a less Old Testament way to reflect grace and not law. God is God and the nature of God is good, peaceful, harmonious, allness expressed and you must be as well. God doesn't throw you out, denounce you, get all irritable or grumpy that you live duality and not oneness with it. It merely means if you are with God you get God, if you are with man you get man. It isn't a jealousy thing at all it is a this or that **not** both.

God knows nothing about you until you open yourself up to it within consciousness and even then God knows nothing of your transgressions because transgressions are of duality and God is to pure to behold inequity ie there is no experiencing both duality and grace at the same time and that is why God cannot know of your earthly experiences to punish you or feel sorry for you.

God is nowhere in the world of man and that is why when you come to God desiring God your history, your human past is wiped away, is no longer *of* you because you are **of** the consciousness of One instead of the consciousness of two and whatever is not of your current state of consciousness, being, expression is no longer your reality; duality is no longer your reality therefore your sins are no longer your reality either rather just the illusion of a past life that has since been corrected.

380.

Dying daily

You cannot put new wine into old skins

Your consciousness cannot be a transparency through which God works while it is double minded. Which Master shall ye serve today? God or Mammon?

381.

You will know pretty soon if you are being "double minded" because your healings will fail, you will see conditions as good and bad and react instead of knowing Truth and dissolving error in your conscious knowing or you begin to encounter karma which had passed you by for a while. Karma isn't punishment from God for disobedience rather it is just an error returning to you to show you the error of you way of being, living, expressing. The sin or erroneous thinking returns upon itself, from where it came and cannot return void for every action has a reaction/karmic return.

382.

God orders your world, it is the guiding, maintaining and sustaining Life and Law of your expression in this form. To know Truth is to purify yourself of the beliefs of man/duality to live under grace but this purification, this clearing of the old consciousness of beliefs must be practiced daily in the form of "dying daily", dissolving errors as they present to you or others. To remain pure, of singular expression, you must keep yourself in the flow of grace which is the expression of God consciousness as your nature of being.

383.

Praying without ceasing:

There must be a principle by which to live, one that is simple, basic and sound that orders all below it into perfect harmony and this is it:

Impersonalization of all good and evil which is the same as not giving reality, validity, emotion, reaction, ie power, to that which doesn't exist knowing that the only power, the only Law, the only Life of you and me is of God, the grace of God, the good of God, completely separate and apart from the good man knows only as the opposite of his bad.

Praying without ceasing is always knowing Truth no matter what presents in your life for validation and acceptance as reality and it isn't *you* that validates or accepts rather **God** revealing itself, **Truth** to you from within.

384.

The mind will be still when it is stayed on God, one power, no confusion, just is. End of conversation. The mind cannot be at rest if there are two or more ways of seeing circumstances, happenings. The mind throws it back and forth; should I or shouldn't I? If this then that, but if this then that. Oh my! The confusion, the turmoil, the thinking ahead to all that could happen if you do, or if you don't. Man is truly the over thinker and in this way cannot be still, cannot rest, cannot find woosaahhh!

The struggle is *mental*, of the thinking mind, and the struggle will prevent you from attaining or achieving that which you are mentally struggling for but if you drop the monkey mind, release it, you are left with spiritual consciousness which is Truth. It is the silent, secret, sacred place where God lives and has its being within you. It is in this quiet receptivity you find your true Self reflected back to you as the image and likeness of the most high, the creator of all, God, good, eternal harmonious expression.

385.

Your desire and receptivity/openness to that which you do not know becomes the resulting consciousness from which you will eventually express as when you know you are **of it.**

386.

I am I am: what it means.

Every person must come to the place of **I am I am.** This is the meaning of the word **mystic,** one in conscious union with God, realized oneness with God and have had the actual experience of God-conscious awareness of its presence within you, felt, communed with, rested upon and prayed to for the things of God-wisdom, peace, patience, benevolence, supply, understanding.

Mysticism is the **practical application,** the living of the principles of this union to bring about a life lived with God as God's expression to the world. Every mystical teaching and every mystic that walks the spiritual path reveals through silent meditation, prayer and treatment that **I am I am,** I am of God and this expresses as harmony, peace, benevolence and ease of being. This is the expression of one who knows God and shares God for the good of all man.

387.

All are of the same household-spiritual-completely furnished and eternal but man tries to make his own household starting from scratch adding sticks and mud to make his stand against the world. This mental short sightedness can be seen as lack and limitation of man vs the allness, wholeness and completeness of God. God is all and you are of the all. When you know this you stop building your stick and mud house and run back to the gilded mansion of the Father.

388.

Just by desiring to be with God in consciousness, have your best friend to learn from and rest in, you are of the nature of this consciousness. This consciousness can be felt as peace, ease, joy, lightness and that expresses out from you to the world as your expression of love, joy, kindness, benevolence etc, to those around you and your being an avenue of expression of God is also the avenue of return of the added things, the perks, the fun, the financial stability, the toys, the perfect pair of boots.

It is backwards to what man's thinking is for man is still the child of want because their constant expression in some form or another is always of lack, *I do not have.* But if you understand you already **are** heir to all that is, all the added things begin to appear to make your experience here on earth the same harmonious and abundant expression of God you feel on the inside.

389.

When you go to a healer you may be seeking the loaves and fishes, the added things, but what the healer is seeking for you is the realization of God, the activity of divine grace and then the added things will be added.

In the beginning patients and students don't realize the visible is not the prize and can be disappointed because they wanted visible, physical, recognizable change for the errors committed by or against them. You only get the outward manifestation of God in form **after** you surrender your *self* to God. After you do this and find it not only a comfortable place to be but a joyous, easy place your outer world begins to change which is an expression of the Truth you know and are living.

390.

Actions speak louder than words. Who you are speaks louder than any word you could utter for the within of you is always expressing who you think you are to the world. That is why there is no reason ever to utter the name of God to another or try to get another to learn about God because just your presence reveals that which is **not of this world** and if they are ready to understand what it is they are feeling they will ask. If you are asked you give milk or meat depending on who is asking ie the consciousness of the person, but if not asked for more you rest in your Truth and bring grace to bear **in the silence** but no outward action is taken to bring God to man through the lips ever unless asked for more.

391.

There is no prison stronger than the prison of belief you **chose** to experience as human man while knowing there is an option that would be your eternal freedom.

392.

The nature of error is illusion.

The moment you perceive there is neither good nor bad, just varying states and stages of conscious awareness, and that your function as a healer is not to remove or heal disease or believe that God heals disease or that there are formulas or rituals or rites or affirmations or idols that will remove disease but to **know** Truth that this whole mortal creation whether it is health or sickness, wealth or poverty, is all made up of the belief that you are separated from God thus suffer what the world throws at you or gloat in what you take first.

One cannot in any way become other than one, it is not divisible and has no opposite, one is one and one **is,** eternal and infinite good. One is harmonious by nature and cannot every be other than harmonious but because man doesn't know his Truth he expresses as he sees fit thus the life man lives is a result of a belief lived as a Truth.

Don't miss out!

Visit the website below and you can sign up to receive emails whenever Kelly Logan publishes a new book. There's no charge and no obligation.

https://books2read.com/r/B-A-KMOW-OHSWI

BOOKS 2 READ

Connecting independent readers to independent writers.

Also by Kelly Logan

365 Days of Truth Volume 1
365 Days of Truth Volume 2
365 Days of Truth Volume 3
Sense to Soul How To Have A Personal Relationship With God Through Mystical Interpretation of Scripture
The Cause and Effect Survival Guide
The Cause And Effect Survival Guide
Intuition: The Best Friend You Didn't Know You Had

Watch for more at www.betterbyintent.com.

About the Author

Kelly A. Logan is an author and contemplative teacher whose work explores the inner experience of God, consciousness, and truth beyond doctrine and tradition. Her writing focuses on direct spiritual awareness, mystical interpretation of scripture, and the quiet transformation that comes from inner listening rather than external authority. She writes for those seeking a personal, lived relationship with God—rooted in clarity, freedom, and direct knowing.

Read more at www.betterbyintent.com.

www.ingramcontent.com/pod-product-compliance
Lightning Source LLC
Chambersburg PA
CBHW021157160426
43194CB00007B/786